Castel Sant'Angelo

Ministero per i Beni e le Attività Culturali
Soprintendenza Speciale per il Polo Museale Romano
Museo Nazionale di Castel Sant'Angelo

Castel Sant'Angelo

Electa

Reprint 2008
First edition 2003

© Ministero per i Beni e le Attività Culturali
Soprintendenza Speciale per il Polo Museale Romano
Museo Nazionale di Castel Sant'Angelo

An editorial realization by Mondadori Electa S.p.A., Milan

www.electaweb.com

This guidebook was produced
by Electa under the supervision
of the Soprintendenza Speciale
per il Polo Museale Romano.

Soprintendente
Claudio Strinati

*Curator of the Museo Nazionale
di Castel Sant'Angelo*
Fiora Bellini

Edited by
Nunzio Giustozzi

Texts
Laura Baini (*L.B.*)
Nunzio Giustozzi (*N.G.*)

Translation
Jeremy Scott

Graphics Coordinator
Dario Tagliabue

Graphic Design
Anna Piccarreta

Page Layout
Chiara Fasoli

Editorial Coordinator
Cristina Garbagna

Editing
Gail Swerling

Technical Coordinators
Paolo Verri
Mario Farè

Contents

ADLOCVTIO
QVADIVINI
TVS IMPVLSI
CONSTANTINI
ANI VICTORIAM
REPERERE

EN TO·YTΩI NIKA.

TWO THOUSAND YEARS OF HISTORY

THE VATICAN AREA IN CLASSICAL ROME

Topography and Archaeological Finds

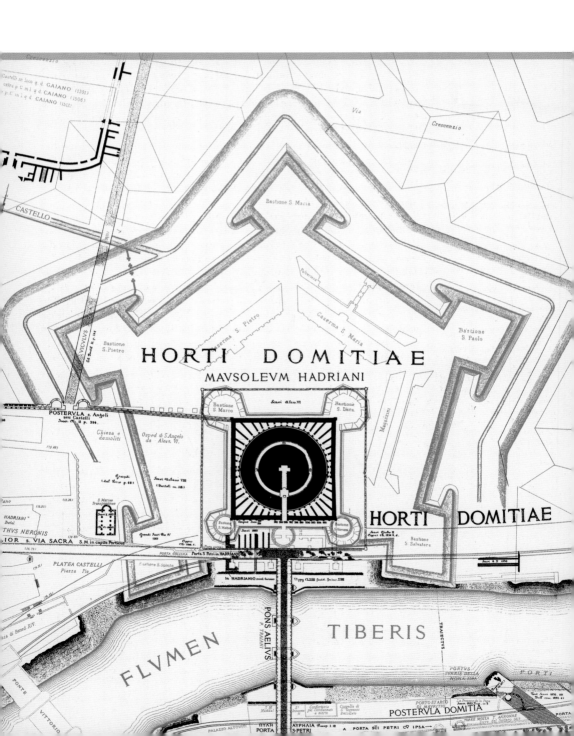

Castel Sant'Angelo stands in what is now one of the central districts of Rome; but when the emperor Hadrian chose this site for his mausoleum, the area lay on the outskirts and was occupied by the tombs erected alongside the roads leaving the city, by imperial and aristocratic villas and gardens, by Roman circuses and by places of worship used by esoteric cults with large followings.

Perhaps deriving from *Vaticum*, an old village in the area, *Ager Vaticanus* was the Roman name for the flat zone which extended from the right bank of the Tiber up to the nearby hills, which were increasingly exploited as a source of the clay used in making bricks. In the Republican era this district was inhabited by artisans and peasants who cultivated vineyards and vegetable gardens—though Cicero does make some unkind comments about the fertility of the soil, and the quality of the wine produced was an easy target for Martial's satire. From Pliny's writings we know that the Vatican was generally viewed as a rather wild area of wasteland, subject to frequent flooding by the Tiber. However, the zone occupied by the modern-day Prati di Castello cannot have been so insalubrious because by the first century BC it was already beginning to fill up with villas, gardens and large public buildings.

The road systems through the area consisted of the Via Cornelia, which used to link Rome to Caere; the Via Triumphalis, which led to Veio across the modern-day Monte Mario; and—in some way that is not entirely clear—of one of the two branches of the Via Aurelia, which ran in the direction of St. Peter's. Stretches of the paving from these highways—and more fragmentary remnants of others roads—have come to light both within modern buildings and just under the level of the present-day streets, making it possible to locate the cross-roads between them at the start of Via della Conciliazione (a side-street leading along the riverside to the mausoleum was uncovered in 1940, suggesting that the road network was extended towards the Pons Aelius after Hadrian's building-work had changed the layout of the area). As was customary in Rome, from the middle of the first century AD onwards those above-mentioned roads leading from the city were lined with tombs (fragments of sarcophagi and tomb inscriptions continue to be discovered here). Some of these tombs were of such imposing size that they became veritable land-marks in the area—for example, the *Meta Romuli* and the *Terebinthus Neronis*. The former, which throughout the Middle Ages was erroneously believed to be the tomb of Scipio Africanus, was over thirty metres high and even bigger than the similarly pyramidal tomb of Caius Cestius, which had been erected when there was a fashion in Rome for things Egyptian and had become known as the *Meta Remi* (hence the contrasting name of the later sepulchre). The foundations of the *Meta Romuli*—together with a large part of the inner walled structure—were unearthed during building-work on the Casa del Pellegrino at the start of Via della Conciliazione, but the only record we have of its actual appearance are medieval and Renaissance views of the area: the building

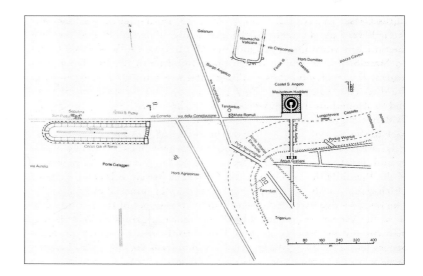

was demolished in 1499 by Pope Alexander VI (Rodrigo Borgia) to make way for his Via Alessandrina, which in its turn would be destroyed to make way for the Via della Conciliazione (the slabs of travertine removed from the tomb were actually used for the floor of St. Peter's Basilica). Probably a victim of the same fate, the *Terebinthus Neronis* stood near the pyramid and the "guide-book" *Mirabilis Urbis Romae* tells us that it was a circular-plan structure consisting of two cylindrical drums one upon the other, almost equalling Hadrian's Mausoleum in height. During the post-war construction of the Auditorium in Via della Conciliazione, the foundations of the *Terebinthus* came to light, and it was discovered that the entire structure must have been enclosed by a vast piazza paved with travertine (part of this paving had already been recuperated in 1564 during the digging work Pius IV had done in the moat around Castel Sant'Angelo). The name of the tomb comes from that of a famous tree which sources say stood in the area and which would later be associated with the martyrdom of St. Peter; this led to the medieval belief that the apostle had been crucified between the two imperial tombs (*inter duas metas*), an idea that was reflected in the paintings of the period—for example, Giotto's representation of the martyrdom in the Stefaneschi triptych now in the Vatican Museum. In that work, an idealised reconstruction of Castel Sant'Angelo, clearly identified with an inscription, is shown on the banks of the Tiber along with the *Meta Remi* (that tomb was in Campo Marzio, hence the personification of Rome holding up an effigy of Mars), the age-old terebinth and the *Meta Romuli*. The crucifixion is actually shown up above (on the Janiculum—perhaps near the site of San Pietro in Montorio?) with a number of horsemen present at the scene and Nero observing the event from the loggia of his palace, probably situated somewhere between the Janiculum and the Vatican. For all its incongruities, this depiction is the product of the artist's attempt to synthesise original sources, the legends of medieval Rome and the first reconstructions of Ancient Rome that were emerging thanks to the work of humanist antiquarians. The result is the creation of a link between the first foundation of Rome and the Christian re-foundation of the city through St. Peter's martyrdom—an idea which obviously provided ideological support for the notion of the papacy's universality.

As far as the urban layout of the entire area is concerned one should mention here the massive—but un-implemented—project put forward by

Julius Caesar in his *Lex de Urbe augenda*, a new town-planning scheme for the coherent development of the entire city. This would have involved the actual re-routing of the Tiber in order to link the Vatican and Campo Marzio, put an end to the constant flooding of the low-lying areas nearest the river, and thus facilitate intensive housing development in the district; as we will see, when constructing his mausoleum Hadrian had to strengthen the drainage systems in the area.

Evidence suggests that actual housing development here can be traced back to the days of Silla: under the hospital of Santo Spirito archaeologists have discovered a fine mosaic floor belonging to a rich villa from that period. Furthermore, we know from Cicero's letters that in the later years of the Republic the area contained numerous private villas and gardens, which would slowly but surely be swallowed up by imperial estates.

The vast area that extended down the northern slopes of the Janiculum as far as the Vatican was occupied by the gardens of Agrippina, wife of Germanicus and mother of Caligula. This is confirmed by written sources—Seneca tells us that the villa was built down towards the river, with hanging gardens on its terraces and porticoes—and by the archaeological evidence

Neo-Attic bowl from Sassia on the banks of the Tiber. Museo Nazionale Romano at the Palazzo Massimo alle Terme, Rome.

M. Cartaro, Plan of the area between Hadrian's Mausoleum and St. Peter's.

The *Sleeping Satyr*, also known as the "Barberini Faun," shown in its present state after the removal of latter additions. Glyptothek, Munich.

that has emerged at various periods in history (unfortunately not always in the most precise circumstances, with no record of the information that is essential if one is to reconstruct the original context of the material found). There are, however, still numerous remains of the complex of buildings that made up the estate; one of the most noteworthy of these was discovered under the Santo Spirito hospital and consists of a brick-built exedra opening onto the river. Another past discovery in this area was an exceptional neo-Attic marble basin from a garden fountain, designed so that the running water gently overflowed the edge and the marine scene carved upon it therefore actually appeared to be underwater. The emergency excavation work carried out during the building of the underground car-park on the Janiculum for the 2000 Jubilee also brought to light various rooms whose walls were frescoed with animal, floral and architectural motifs; from the building techniques used, one could date that complex to the second century AD, the period when the villa was enjoying its greatest splendour.

Having inherited the estate after the dramatic death of his mother, Caligula had a private chariot-track created on what is now the site of St. Peter's. To adorn the *spina*—the central wall which ran down the middle of the circuit—the emperor imported an imposing Egyptian obelisk; the only one to remain standing after the demise of the Roman empire, this was subsequently moved to the centre of St. Peter's Square. For his part, Nero is known to have carried out restoration work on the villa in which, following the disastrous fire of 64 AD that destroyed two-thirds of the housing on the other side of the Tiber, he provided shelter for tens of thousands of Romans. And it was in the nearby gardens—known throughout the Middle Ages as "the meadows of Nero"—that this emperor, who was determined to crush nascent Christianity, had the Christians accused of setting the fire either crucified or burnt alive, offering the Romans a macabre spectacle of "nocturnal illuminations," This was the period of persecution during which Peter himself was martyred.

Nero was also the emperor who linked the imperial grounds with Campo Marzio on the other side of the river by building (or perhaps restor-

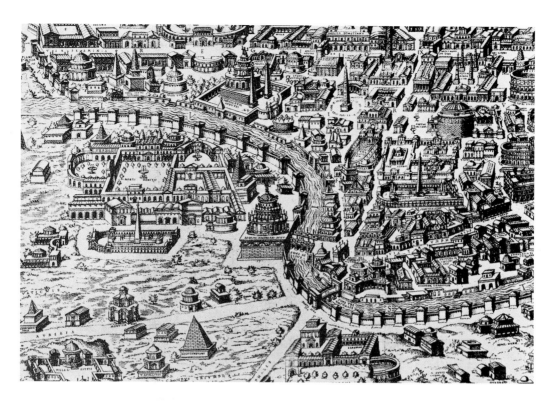

ing) the *Pons Triumphalis* (named after the road which starts there); during extreme low water in the Tiber one can still see some of the piers of this structure a few metres downstream from the modern-day Ponte Vittorio Emanuele II. In fact, during construction work on that nineteenth-century bridge, fragments of a bronze statue and of marble parapets came to light, suggesting that perhaps the *Pons Neronianus* had been as magnificent in decoration as Hadrian's *Pons Aelius*.

However, Nero was not the only one in *Ager Vaticanus* to possess an estate with avenues, porticoes and pleasure pavilions. The area stretching from the site Hadrian chose for his mausoleum to that of the present-day Palazzo di Giustizia [Court House] was occupied by the gardens of Domitia, who some—on the basis of an inscription found at Castel Sant'Angelo—identify as Longina, the wife of Domitian, and others with Nero's aunt Lepida (whom, according to Suetonius, the emperor had murdered so he could lay his hands on her property). Part of the sculptural adornments of the *Horti Domitiae* must have been the famous statue of the *Sleeping Satyr*, which is perhaps an original Greek work dating from around 220 BC and was subsequently brought to light in the Castel Sant'Angelo moat during the excavation work commissioned by Pope Urban VIII in 1624–28 to strengthen the fortifications. This masterpiece, which was repaired by Bernini (for whom it was undoubtedly a source

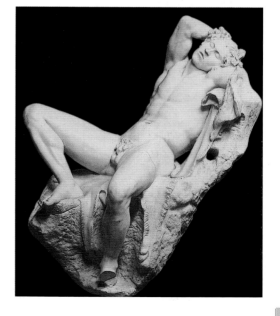

of inspiration) and then later by Pacetti, was for many years part of the Palazzo Barberini collection until, after long negotiations, it was sold to Prince Ludwig of Baveria for the Munich Glyptothek. The statue could not—as some have argued—have been part of the decoration of the mausoleum; it must have adorned first a sumptuous Greek home and then, at some point, have been brought to Rome, where again it formed part of a lavish domestic decor. Powerful and untamed, brimming with youthful energy, the figure was intended for a setting of greenery and water: the water-spout for a fountain emerged from the hole drilled in the marble just under the left arm. And whilst its surroundings suggested the world of Nature, the sprawling, recumbent satyr suggested ideas of total physical abandonment in a work which, for the ancient viewer, will have conjured up Dionysian notions of inebriation, ecstasy and sensual pleasure.

During building-work on the Castel Sant'Angelo side of the Palazzo di Giustizia, sizeable structures in the *Horti Domitiae* came to light—perhaps the remnants of a long portico of columns with refined capitals in polychrome marble. More recent excavation work, during the construction of the Castello underpass to the east of Hadrian's Mausoleum, has brought to light a lot of ceramic work, painted plaster-work and marble slabs with plant volute decoration—all of which probably came from richly-decorated buildings within the gardens.

Here again, sizeable areas were set aside for the construction of tombs. One remarkable discovery under the Court House was that of the sarcophagus of the eighteen-year-old girl, Crepereia Tryphena, whose rich tomb furnishings included various archaeological gems—most strikingly, an ivory doll with articulated limbs and a complicated hairstyle that dates from the Antonine period. Lanciani's description of the find still conveys all the amazement it caused: "Having removed the lid and glanced in at the body, we were strangely surprised by the appearance of the skull, which still seemed to be covered with a dense head of long hair floating to and fro in the water." The exhumation of the young girl took place with solemn honours amidst a crowd of onlookers. Other majestic buildings of pagan Rome in the *Ager Vaticanus* area included the *Gaianum*—perhaps "the enclosure"—where Caligula practised with his *biga* [two-horsed-chariot], and the *Naumachia*, built for displays of naval warfare by Trajan (its remains have been identified in the area to the north of Hadrian's Mausoleum).

Nevertheless, given its position outside the urban area proper, this zone was also seen as suitable for the ritual worship associated with the various salvatory religions of eastern origin which were so popular amongst the freed slaves working on the imperial estates. Source material, extant inscriptions and archaeological evidence reveal the presence here of an important sanctuary dedicated to the Phrygian goddess Cybele, and of sites holy to Mithras and Apollo. In effect, during the second and third centuries AD the Vatican area was an important centre for solar worship, given that part of the emperor Hadrian's full title was "Apollineus of Aelius" and the mausoleum itself—the temple of deified emperors—played a part in this veneration of the Sun. Even after the advent of Christianity, solar ideas remained strong: Christ was referred to as the *Sol Novus* and often represented with the attributes that had pre-

viously been associated with Apollo (symbols which would frequently figure in the decoration of Christian tombs). However, the establishment of Christianity did mean that the basilica raised in the name of the apostle martyred by Nero became the central monument in the entire area, pushing even Hadrian's imposing mausoleum into the background—a fact which, as Paolo Liverani points out, delighted the heart of St. Augustine, who makes emphatic mention of it in the account of his visit to Rome in 404 during the days of emperor Honorius. But as is well-known, in the Middle Ages Castel Sant'Angelo would find a new role, becoming the bulwark of the whole *Ager Vaticanus*, an area which was not enclosed by walls until the ninth century, after the Saracens had sacked the Vatican Basilica.

"Kings come to Rome [...] Here is the tomb of the fisherman, there is the temple of the emperor. Peter is here in the tomb, Hadrian is there in the temple. The temple of Hadrian, the 'memory' of Peter. The emperor came, and we see which concerned him most, where he decided to bend his knee: in the temple of the emperor or to the memory of the fisherman? He set aside his diadem and beat his breast in the place where lies the body of the fisherman..." ~ ST. AUGUSTINE OF HIPPO ~

What is more, the architecture and very concept of the mausoleum would influence the various designs drawn up for new St. Peter's by Bramante, Raphael, Peruzzi and Antonio da Sangallo. The dome, which originally was to be surrounded by a drum of columns—modelled on the *tholoi* of Classical architecture—was intended to reconstruct the imposing mass of the ancient structure: even at a visual level, the Vatican basilica was, therefore, to be the mausoleum of the second Rome, the imperial tomb of Peter and his successors (Julius II saw himself as both a new Caesar and a new Augustus). More than any other part of the city, this combination of Tiber, Vatican and imperial tomb gives one a sense of the bond that has existed for two thousand years between the world of pagan antiquity and the world of a new humanity reborn in Christ. (*N.G.*)

HADRIAN'S MAUSOLEUM

Historical sources contain numerous mentions of the frequent attempts that were made to destroy the mausoleum entirely or—in periods of poverty and need—strip it of structural and decorative material that could be used for humbler building work. These continual depradations, which actually started in the days of Classical Antiquity, gradually obliterated many of the salient architectural features of the tomb that Hadrian had built for himself and his family, so that by the Middle Ages the monument was—like the Campidoglio or the Roman Forum—little more than a ruin: before the advent of Pope Boniface IX at the end of fourteenth century, it was actually being used as grazing-land for sheep. However, the earliest remaining medieval additions to the structure—at what is now the level of the internal courtyards, but was originally the upper level of the Roman stone drum—date from the beginning of the Middle Ages. After all, how could one ignore the convenient foundations proved by such a massive structure, which was both well-built and located in a strategic position? Perhaps it is precisely due to the construction work which has accumulated around it that one owes the conservation of the more ancient structures; as with another of Hadrian's buildings in Rome—the Pantheon—almost constant use (even if for very different purposes) guaranteed the necessary continuity in maintenance that enabled what was left of the archaeological monument to survive.

The papal fortress may not retain the original volume of the structure, but it did make only slight alterations to its height; however, within modern Rome, Castel Sant'Angelo is not the imposing presence it once was, being partly screened by the Palazzo di Giustizia and the surrounding urban fabric; and just like the Tiber itself, the wonderful bridge which serves to nuance the solid mass from which it projects, is practically invisible unless one is on the river bank. In Roman times, the mausoleum must have made a very different impression; dominating as it did the flat lands around it, the building was an imposing presence both for those travelling along the river and those looking across from the other bank. Hadrian's choice of the site was no accident, given that he intended his sepulchre to be a compelling expression both of the Greek culture with which he himself was so thoroughly imbued and of the knowledge he had acquired from his extensive travels through the provinces of the Roman Empire. Constantly troubled by thoughts of death, the emperor was anxious not only to guarantee his "line" but also to leave posterity a clear memory of himself; and as someone who had dedicated so much trouble to the restoration of the tombs of Pompey and of the Theban general Epaminondas, he must have given considerable thought to exactly where he wanted this monument to stand. Eccentric by nature, he chose to go against the tradition, dating back at least as far as the first century BC, which made Campo Marzio the burial ground of the Roman elite (however, as we shall see, the Augustan mausoleum that stood not far from there would be one of his most obvious inspirations). The decision to opt for an area which was removed from the hustle and bustle of city life

Hadrian's Mausoleum,
atmospheric view
of the helicoidal ramp
(photo A. De Luca).

and yet was already imperial property would seem to reveal a desire to establish some sort of distance between himself and Rome, a city whose hostility and criticisms he had been on the receiving end of. However, he also needed to maintain some contact with that city, and this was guaranteed by the *Pons Aelius*: during the building phase, the bridge was useful for the transport of materials, and thereafter made an important contribution to the finished structure by emphasising the approach to it. The choice of the right bank of the Tiber could also have been determined by religious considerations of Graeco-Oriental origin, something which would seem to be borne out by Maria Maddalena Alessandro's recent reading of the cosmological significance of the layout and architecture of the building and its association with the waters of the river. Such symbolism would explain the decision to build on a site which may have been solid but still required the creation of extensive drainage works to guarantee the stability of the final structure.

We do not know exactly when building work began, though perhaps it was around 130 AD; however, some stamped bricks discovered in the construction date back to 123 AD, which is actually before the above-mentioned drainage work on the sub-foundations. What is certain is that the mausoleum was not finished in 138 AD, when Hadrian died at Baiae (near Naples) and had to be provisionally buried in Pozzuoli, at the villa which had once belonged to Cicero. The inauguration of the mausoleum would come the following year when, having completed the building, the emperor Antoninus Pius had the earthly remains of his predecessor buried there after cremation; according to Filippo Coarelli, the *ustrinum* used to cremate the bodies of Hadrian and his wife, Sabina, is to be identified with the monument discovered in the late nineteenth century in Piazza Sforza.

The last ashes to be deposited in the earlier mausoleum of Augustus had been those of Nerva (who died in 98 AD), whilst the urn with the remains of Trajan and his wife Plotina had been buried at the base of the famous Column to which that emperor gives his name. From now on, for more than a century, Hadrian's Mausoleum would be the tomb of the Roman emperors, the burial place of not only Hadrian and his wife, but also: Lucius Helius Caesar, his adopted son; Antoninus Pius, a fine portrait of him from inside the mausoleum is still to be seen in the Castle museum; Antoninus' wife, Faustina, and his son Lucius Verus; the philosopher/emperor Marcus Aurelius (perhaps); Commodus; Septimius Severus; Julia Domna, her son Geta, and other members of the Antonine family, whose presence in the tomb would lead to it becoming known as *Sepulcrum Antoniorum*. The last emperor we know for certain to have been buried there was Caracalla, assassinated by his legionaries in 217 AD. However, the mausoleum may have gone on receiving the bodies of his successors right up to 403 AD, when—in the reign of Honorius—it was included in the Aurelian Walls and made into a sort of bulwark defending the right bank of the river and the city beyond. It is likely that as early as the reign of Aurelian (271 AD), the mausoleum was modified to serve as a fortress—that is, long before the much more obvious alterations it would undergo during the Middle Ages. After all, it is highly improbable that the entire Vatican region was left without defences, and that such a structure was left to fall into the hands of an enemy who could thence attack from above the inhabited areas lying beyond the natural defensive barrier formed by the bend in the river. By fortifying the position themselves, the Romans would have created a commanding forward position from which to strike back at armies whose advance southwards to the "Meadows of Nero" was practically unhindered.

Within pagan Rome, the mausoleum competed with the Coliseum and the Pantheon in majesty and elegance, and may have been designed by the emperor himself, who was not new to such architectural challenges (think, for example, of Hadrian's Villa). However, we still have no very clear idea of the form and decoration of the original structure, due to the continual additions—and subtractions—made over the course of the centuries. That difficulty is particularly clear in the upper part; this suffered most when the structure was converted into a papal residence and none of the innumerable theories put forward as to its original appearance have yet been confirmed beyond any reasonable doubt. The overall structure was a skilful composition of parallel-sided and cylindrical volumes raised upon each other, with the various levels characterised by different circumferences or linear perimeters. In front of the mausoleum stood bronze gates fixed to pilasters resting on peperino foundations; work on the Tiber embankment in 1891–92 unearthed not only these foundations, but also the travertine threshold and two pilasters which stood at the entrance and probably supported gilded bronze peacocks (symbols of immortality, two of these latter have survived and can now be seen in the Cortile della Pigna in the Vatican). The enclosure wall ran around a brick-built base that stood 15 meters high and formed an 89-metre square, which—for reasons we do not know—was added immediately after the completion of the structure. Within that base were radial walls that ran from around the drum, forming long vaulted enclosures that were surmounted by terraces. The outer walls were faced in slabs of white marble framed by pilaster strips decorated with a frieze of festoons and *bucrania* [ox skulls]; fragments of these can now be seen in the Castle Museum. Procopius tells us that at the four corners of the basement stood bronze sculptural groups of men and horses—perhaps works that Hadrian had brought from Greece or the Middle East—whilst the different levels of the south-facing river front, which included the monumental entrance with its triple barrel vault, were decorated with marble plaques bearing the epitaphs of the imperial personages buried within the mausoleum. The actual inscriptions are only known to us from documents, given that the slabs themselves were barbarically destroyed when, in 1579, Pope Gregory XIII had them removed and sawn into sections to adorn the Gregorian Chapel in St. Peter's. Another pope—Alexander VI—had by that point already ripped away the bronze door and the epigraphs of Hadrian and Sabina that surmounted the large arch which formed the entrance to the monument (three metres beneath the level of the present entrance).

Immediately opposite the entrance stood the large cylinder of the mausoleum proper, which now forms the lower part of the Castle: 21 metres high and 64 metres in diameter, it was in rough-mix concrete [*opus incertum*]

Model of the original appearance of Hadrian's Mausoleum. Museo Nazionale di Castel Sant'Angelo.

Model of the Romanic structure of Hadrian's Mausoleum without subsequent additions. Museo Nazionale di Castel Sant'Angelo.

faced with blocks of tufa, peperino and travertine, and an outer covering of marble slabs; it may also have had pilaster strips and been surmounted by statues. What remains of the drum is its massive inner core, with just some remnants of the precious stone facing (most of which had already been stripped away in ancient times). The central vaulted corridor (*dromos*) is, however, well preserved. Made of precisely-aligned blocks of travertine, it leads to a square atrium, where a large semicircular apse in the end wall would seem once to have housed a colossal statue of Hadrian (only the head has survived, and can now be seen in the Rotunda of the Vatican museum). One other niche—this time rectangular—opens on the left side of the vestibule, forming part of a Greek cross layout that was similar to that observed in shrines to Mithras; as one can see from the holes for the metal brackets, all the walls were faced with ancient yellow (Numidian?) marble. On the right begins the helicoidal ramp that is a characteristic feature of the structure, running up to the next level in one complete circuit of the cylinder. The ramp passageway, three metres wide and six high, has a dry-stone vault and for one stretch brick cambering; it was perhaps faced with stucco. Parts of the white mosaic of the original floor are still visible, though mainly one now sees the underlying *opus signinum* [compressed rubble]. The walls must have originally been faced with marble up to a height of three metres, where a uniform groove has been interpreted as the fitting for a cornice. However, the brickwork itself is of such a quality that it would have been a shame to cover it, with compact, non-porous walls, neatly lodged mortar and—at regular intervals of 1.20 metres—what appear to be decorative bands of bipedal bricks (that is, bricks that were a "double foot" in size: 60 × 60 cm). Four vertical shafts in the vault provide light and air, and may also have served to collect rain water, which was then carried away by a gutter that runs under the ramp. It has been argued that the openings had an important functional role during the building stage—for the raising of materials from one level to the other—but it is more evocative to view them as telescopes focused on the heavens above. They are in fact aligned with the four cardinal points of the compass (M.M. Alessandro). One hundred and twenty-five metres of ramp brings one through 360° and up a dozen metres from the atrium, then it leads into a corridor that runs the diameter of the drum (like the entrance *dromos*) into the large room that stands at the centre of the monument and probably housed the earthly remains of the emperor. The present-day incline—a graded ramp created in the last years of the fifteenth century by Pope Alexander VI—changes the perception of what should have been the final approach to the funeral chamber (which like the atrium has a layout which recalls that of mithraea). Eight metres square, that sepulchral *cella* still remains austere and solemn in spite of the changes that have been made over the centuries. However, we cannot get a full idea of the grandiose space, given that it is broken lengthways by the Valadier bridge (once a drawbridge), nor can we possibly imagine the richness of the original decor. Today, two large air-vent windows at the sides of the barrel vault admit unintended amounts of light into the room, whose un-mortared walls are made of precisely-cut blocks of travertine with three arched rectangular niches (two to the sides, one at the end) for the cinerary urns of Hadrian, Sabina and Helius Caesar. A strip of coloured marble still attached to the north wall reveals that the room must originally have been faced—walls and floor—with such precious materials (as a socle of peperino around the entire space shows, that floor must have been slightly higher than what one sees now).

The Urn Chamber is surmounted by the two or three rooms at different levels, which are all that now remains of the Roman tower, the fulcrum of the architectural appearance and static equilibrium of the whole complex:

remnants of the walls and layout of these original rooms can be seen from the Theatre Courtyard and Courtyard of Honour, east and west of the main block. Even the most recent archaeological studies have not been able to identify how these upper levels were reached; nowadays, access to the tower is solely via rooms and corridors that mainly date from the sixteenth century. In layout, the Chamber of Justice is broadly similar to the Urn Chamber below; built of un-mortared stone blocks, it must initially have been very high, given that the fresco on the north wall appears to have been cut away at the top. In its turn, the lowered barrel vault of this room serves to support the much higher, domed rotunda above, the Treasure Chamber. Here, behind the wood shelving that dates from the first half of the sixteenth century one can still make out the Roman brick wall-facing with its load-bearing arches. Above, the tower must have ended in a fourth room enclosed by a narrow elliptical corridor, which served to reach the top of the mausoleum and is still visible today: as one can see from the parts left unplastered, the interior of the Roman structure is substantially intact. Unfortunately, there are no Roman descriptions of what topped off the sepulchre. Probably, the space between the cylindrical drum and the square structure emerging from it was filled with earth and laid out as a hanging garden. This may also have served as the podium for the colossal bronze statues of Hadrian and of the four-horse chariot driven by Helios: the—still debated—representation on a coin minted during the reign of Antonius Pius, together with a reference by Cassius Dion and a story told by John of Antioch (eighth century), would all suggest these once occupied the position where now stands the angel that gives the mausoleum its modern name. The layout of the upper part of the monument is undoubtedly circular, which suggests that the outward decoration was also cylindrical and probably consisted of a colonnade. It is also possible that the structure beneath was another cylindrical drum, even if the room within it is square in ground-plan: after all, the Urn Chamber and the Vestibule are Greek Cross even though contained within a circular structure. Hence, it would appear that the mausoleum was made up of a square basement supporting three cylinders of diminishing diameters—rather like a wedding cake—and that it was probably enclosed with colonnades or had niches for statues. This can be surmised from the irregularities to be seen in the outer surface of the one drum that has survived. The pre-existing Roman structures obviously had to be "rectified" so that they could be incorporated within later additions, and architectural features such as colonnades, friezes and sculpture—which made up a far from solid external surface—would undoubtedly have been easy to remove. (N.G.)

Hadrian's Mausoleum, plan of the southern side. The structures that are part of Castel Sant'Angelo are traced in dotted lines (from Coarelli 1994).

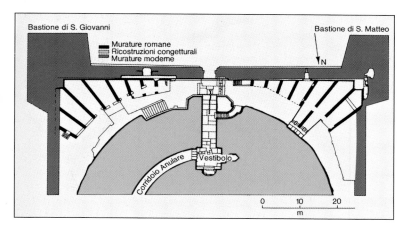

Augustus' Mausoleum
as it is today and in the
reconstruction proposed
by G. Gatti in 1938.

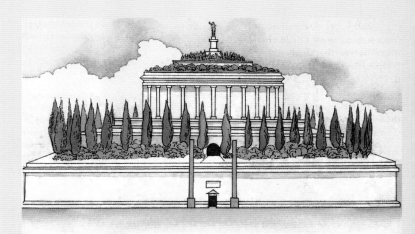

From Pirro Ligorio to Piranesi, the plans and paintings of Ancient Rome always show Hadrian's Mausoleum in relation to that of Augustus, the grandiose tomb built some one hundred and fifty years earlier, thus underlining that this sepulchre of the *gens Iulia* was the later emperor's inspiration for the monument intended to celebrate his own dynasty. According to Cesare D'Onofrio, a true expert on Rome, the similarity between certain measurements and proportions in the two structures cannot have been accidental. Made up of five concentric circular walls, the *Augusteum* had a maximum diameter of 87 metres and stood 12 metres high, whilst the square wall enclosure for the *Hadrianeum* measured more than 86 metres and stood 12 metres tall; hence, the base structure of the latter makes clear reference to the former. What is more, the *Augusteum* comprises two distinct architectural components: the external circular base, and the inner—and much higher—drum surmounted by a statue of the emperor; as Strabo records, the two were linked by a dense crown of evergreens (cypresses?). Borgatti suggested that Hadrian's Mausoleum adopted the same idea, with sloping surfaces of earth steps which Hülsen argued linked the top of the cylinder to the structure which crowned it. Furthermore, the deep analogies between the two buildings are said to be confirmed by the fact that Italic-Etruscan tumuli tombs were the inspiration for both. Piles of earth were certainly found during restoration work under the floor of the papal apartments (beneath the level of a room alongside the oil and grain storerooms dating from the time of Alexander VI) and under the Cortile dell'Angelo, but doubts raised as to whether these date from Roman times mean one cannot confirm the claim that there was a hanging garden here. What is more, Marisa De' Spagnolis has quite rightly underlined how the Etruscan-Italic cumuli may have fitted in with the conservative ideology being proposed by Augustus, but Hadrian's tastes in both art and architecture were much more influenced by Greek culture; and for her part, Elena Calandra has argued that the undeniable analogies between the two mausolea are in fact to be traced back to the dynastic architecture of the East—more

Coin of the second century AD showing a pyre surmounted by a symbolic quadriga (or is it Hadrian's Mausoleum?). The structure of the pyre—on which a dead emperor was deified through the cremation of his mortal remains—may have influenced the design of the mausoleum.

specifically, the mausoleum of Halicarnassus and of Alexander the Great; though there seems little chance that we will ever know what the latter looked like, it is true that the former of the two monuments did provide the very name "mausoleum" for the opulent circular-plan tombs of imperial Christian families (the term was only applied to the *Sepulcrum Hadriani* or *Antoninorum* in the seventeenth century, after it had become a *castellum*).

Another clear source of inspiration for Hadrian could have been the *pyrae*, those layered wooden structures which were used in the cremation and deification of emperors (as we can see from coins issued under Herodianus in the third century AD, these could comprise as many a five different levels). Tina Squadrilli too would support the, yet to be confirmed, claim that the image on the back of the *consecratio* coins of Antoninus Pius, minted after Hadrian's death and—more importantly—after the completion of the tomb, does not depict a generic "pyre" but the original structure of the mausoleum (which at this point would, contrary to the descriptions that have come down to us, appear to have consisted of four sections). (*N.G.*)

Leon Battista Alberti,
View of the Mausoleum,
from *De Re Aedificatoria*,
VIII, 3.

Andrea Mantegna, west wall
of the *Camera Picta*, 1474,
detail of the fresco.
Castello di San Giorgio,
Mantua.

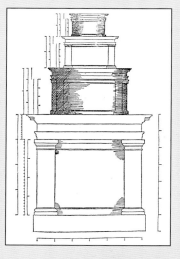

A building rich in associations and symbolism, the mausoleum as it appears nowadays is the result of sizeable alterations in structure and function. These changes mean that the original form of the building is largely unknown to us, and such uncertainty has resulted in the proliferation of—often unreliable—descriptions which have been an inexhaustible source of inspiration for all types of imaginative reconstructions from the fifteenth century onwards.

Figuring in the background of numerous history paintings and pictorial maps of Rome, the mausoleum served as a very image of the city itself; however, some did take a more scholarly, antiquarian approach to the depiction of this mysterious structure. One early representation appears in a late-fourteenth-century fresco in the church of San Francesco in Arezzo, which shows the procession held by Pope Gregory the Great in 590 to free the city of a terrible plague. Here one sees the miraculous appearance of the Archangel Michael on a small square tower surmounting a mausoleum which is made up of three—still predominantly Classical—components above an outsized base. Some medieval features are however visible—for example, the single light windows and the pensile arches—and such architectural syncretism is probably an indication that the process of conversion from tomb to fortress had already begun. This can also be seen in the panel that Filarete modelled for the bronze door of St. Peter's (1439–45), where the bas-relief shows the mausoleum as three/four sections placed one on top of the other, in line with the simple reading of the structure that Leon Battista Alberti gave in his *De Re Aedificatoria*. The depiction here comprises: a square base with rustication, corner pilasters surmounted by capitals and a crowning frieze with festoons and *bucrania*; a drum with rustication and a similar cornice as well as a colonnade; and a culminating body of uncertain ground-plan—perhaps circular, perhaps square—with a second peristyle surmounted by a small cupola crowned by a statue (the picturesque figure at the half-open door in the base is a quotation of an image that often appears on ancient sarcophagi and serves to underline the former use of the building).

The image that appears in the frieze to the marble altarpiece in the Salviati Chapel of San Gregorio al Celio in Rome dates from slightly later; it shows pilaster strips rather than columns and the statue on the conic pinnacle is recognisable as the Archangel Michael, at whose appearance Gregory the Great and his court fall to their knees. The subject also appears in a similar type of composition within the predella of the altarpiece of *Madonna and Saints* painted by Matteo di Giovanni in Siena around 1479.

Archaeological interest in Hadrian's Mausoleum also began to make itself felt in Northern Italy by the fifteenth century. Mantegna's various depictions of the ancient world include a large circular building on a high base, a fantastic construction that suggests some sort of knowledge of the Augustan and Hadrian mausolea (the latter probably the inspiration for the high base); in the background behind the putti holding a plaque with dedicatory inscription over one of the two doorways in the *Camera degli Sposi*, the artist could not resist the temptation to give a complete—and therefore partially imaginary—image of the famous monument.

I have also referred to the sculptor Filarete's taste for the Classical Antiquity; but that world would also become a common point of reference thanks to the Greek humanism of Philelphus, vividly recorded in the travel notebooks of Ciriaco Pizzecolli (Ciriaco d'Ancona) which enjoyed a great vogue in the cultural circles of the Po valley. One cannot, therefore, rule out Saxl's suggestion that the image of Castel Sant'Angelo on Filarete's bronze door is to be linked with a reconstruction of the monument offered by Pizzecolli himself. Fifteenth-century "records" of the appearance of the mausoleum were closely bound up with contemporary cartography, given that the monument was frequently used as a topographical point of reference. Filarete, however, seems to have been the first to offer an antiquarian reconstruction of its original appearance, perhaps taking his inspiration from a fragment of the ancient enclosure which contained a depiction of the Castel Sant'Angelo as seen from the Borgo side (it was reproduced in the *Codex Escurialensis*). The same archaeological approach to Classical Antiquity can be seen in the imaginative illustrations in the *Marcanova Codex* which show the Castle as it actually appeared at the time of Nicholas V, the pope who had commissioned considerable work on the structure (his coat-of-arms can still be seen in the middle of the lower tower). This folio, along with the others that Hülsen used at the beginning of the twentieth century to illustrate Ciriaco de' Pizzecolli's vision of Ancient Rome, is partly based on a sketch from life. The Ponte Sant'Angelo is shown with its five openings and the crenellated medieval towers which guarded the approaches from Campo Marzio and Borgo; and in the background is a landscape with castles and ruins. The mausoleum basement is shown with its ancient rustication, Corinthian corner pilasters and frieze with garlands (however, these are strung between putti heads, not the *bucrania* that appear in the more exact drawings by such sixteenth-century architects as Antonio and Giuliano

Giovanni Marcanova,
*Hadrian's Mausoleum and
the Ponte Sant'Angelo*, 1465.
Biblioteca Estense, Modena.
This parchment illustration
is particularly important
because it shows the statue of
the angel with the sword in its
right hand, which had been
raised on the top of the Castle
just twenty years earlier.

Antonio Labacco, *Imaginary
Reconstruction of Hadrian's
Mausoleum*, 1552, engraving.
Museo Nazionale di Castel
Sant'Angelo.

Giovan Battista Piranesi
Frontispiece to *Campus Martius
Antiquae Urbis Romae*. Istituto
Nazionale per la Grafica,
Rome.

Emile Vaudremer
Reconstruction of the Mausoleum.
École des Beaux-Arts, Paris.

da Sangallo and Jacopo Sansovino). Even the image of the monument that appears in the Farnese apartments within Castel Sant'Angelo itself strike one as heavily idealised and a long way from what must have been its original appearance, whilst the plan drawn up by Sallustio Peruzzi does show both the central core and its seven radials; for all its inexactitude, this latter work reveals that nascent taste for archaeological study of the surviving structure which would be the basis for the hypotheses about the appearance of the original mausoleum advanced in the centuries to come. Labacco's interpretation was the first to comprise the now-accepted idea of three sections, one on top of the other, with a line of statues crowning the top of the drum, the four sculptural groups of figures at the corners of the base, and the pine cone at the very summit of the edifice. From this point onwards, suggestions throughout the sixteenth and seventeenth century would follow this model, though with some variations and it was not really until the nineteenth century that the architect Canina was able to draw on the evidence provided by recent archaeological discoveries to offer a synthesis of all the previous hypotheses as to the original appearance of the mausoleum. Nevertheless, on-site study of the Roman ruins had been at the basis of the numerous engravings of Castel Sant'Angelo and its bridge produced by Giovan Battista Piranesi at different phases in his artistic career. The extraordinary 1756 etching of *View of the Foundations of Hadrian's Mausoleum*, now in the Castel Sant'Angelo Museum, reveals just how much representations of the structure had already changed: the aim was no longer to suggest what the original might have been like but rather to depict the extant ancient structure, stripped of all subsequent accretions and modifications. However, even Piranesi could not resist the lure of imagination, and the frontispiece of his collection *Campo Marzio in Ancient Rome* shows an exaggeratedly high mausoleum drum adorned with a different architectural order at each level and crowned with two rather odd arches—the whole set within an imaginative composition of obelisks and majestic colonnades. Another work that is of little archaeological exactitude but great atmospheric effect is the famous image produced by Emile Vaudremer during his period of study at the Académie de France in Rome, a necessary stopping-point for all those doing the classical "Grand Tour." The rarefied atmosphere of the picture captures the silent passage of time; and in his depiction of the monument, with its tapering, stepped cone leading up to the gold quadriga driven by Helios or Apollo, the French architect has clearly taken his inspiration from the tomb of Mausolus. As André Chastel so appositely points out, during the French Revolution the mausoleum became the model for the "Elysée or public cemetery"; in effect, this would be the first period of history since the second century AD to reveal a clear obsession with large public buildings dedicated to death, edifices that were seen as "sublime as the mountains full of untroubled ghosts." The drawings produced then of possible tombs for the most illustrious and wise are still very atmospheric and incorporate various designs: a circular three-storey structure with rather stiff-looking columns seen against the sky, or lines of cypresses planted densely in front of arcades that were to be divided into locules to hold the ashes of the greatest possible number of *citoyens* and *citoyennes*…

This long series of fanciful depictions may well have played a primary role in making Hadrian's Mausoleum one of the most famous extant monuments of Classical Rome. However, it ultimately came to an end in 1890, when Christian Hülsen proposed a reconstruction which, in spite of a few incongruities, is substantially comparable to that accepted as probable by modern archaeologists and scholars. (*N.G.*)

Possible reconstruction of the decoration of the square basement of the mausoleum (from Strong 1953).

Corinthian-style pilaster capital from Hadrian's Mausoleum. Museo Nazionale di Castel Sant'Angelo.

Marble slab decorated with garland and *bucranium*, from the outer decoration of the drum. Museo Nazionale di Castel Sant'Angelo.

A Monument Stripped Bare: The Sculptural Decoration of the Mausoleum

Reference has already been made to the fact that over the centuries the mausoleum was stripped of materials for re-use in buildings both inside Rome and beyond: for example, fairly reliable sources tell us that seven marble works were taken to Orvieto to adorn the famous Duomo. Thus not only a large part of the architectural structure has disappeared but also most of its rich decoration—almost nothing is left of the prized marble wall panels or the sculptural works that adorned it both inside and outside. However, careful study of the pieces left *in situ*, of the most famous marble works known to have come from the mausoleum, and of the fragments now in the Castle storerooms, has enabled archaeologists to work towards a reconstruction of the original appearance of the monument. In her recent critical discussion of the sculptural decoration, Maria Antonietta Tomei accepts as still valid the reconstruction of the square basement put forward by Strong in the 1950s, evidence in support of which comes from some drawings and notes in Giuliano da Sangallo's sketchbooks, which were made when the facing of the south-west corner was partly intact and various other fragments still survived. The only extant pieces of that original decoration are small parts of the architrave comprising two smooth bands and decorated mouldings—now in the Boniface IX Ambulatory, walled in around the base of the mausoleum drum—whilst a substantial part of the upper cornice, comprising lions' heads interspersed with elegant palmettes, was reused atop the three medieval Ionic columns that adorn a house in Via del Banco del Santo Spirito (their origin is proved by the existence of similar fragments in the Castle storerooms). The reconstruction of the frieze, which source drawings show as comprising bulls' heads and garlands surmounted with *paterae* [sacrificial plates], is more problematic. For example, the large block of bas-relief with a similar motif which was unearthed in front of the Castle in 1891 cannot have come from the decoration of the square basement: it is bigger than the other similar fragments discovered during excavation work, is decorated with shields where there should be *paterae*, and has a curved back surface (though, it has been argued, this is due to the piece having been adapted so that it could be used to decorate the top of the cylindrical tower between the bridge and the mausoleum built at the time of Alexander VI). What is more probable is that the harmonious decoration of the *Hadrianeum* had two very similar friezes: the smaller one running around the walls of the square base, the larger one around the top of the drum; this would seem to be borne out by Filarete's panel in the bronze door of St. Peter's and a drawing by Fra' Giocondo.

Even more recent studies have not been able to identify the original location of other fragments of architectural decoration with any great certainty. For example, the refined Corinthian-style capital from a non-weight-bearing corner pilaster—found near the Castel Sant'Angelo and now to be seen in the covered walkway commissioned by Pius IV—could have adorned the south-west corner of the basement or have been part of the interior decor.

The numerous catalogued fragments include column bases, cornices, cor-

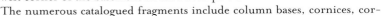

Maestro dell'Ala di Uccello,
Castel Sant'Angelo, 1546–53.
engraving. Museo Nazionale
di Castel Sant'Angelo. This
clearly shows the frieze with
festoons and bulls' skulls
that the Borgia pope used
to decorate the tower built
between the bridge and
mausoleum.

bels, candelabra and fragments of architrave and strip pilasters which are not easy to identify. More sizeable extant features are the columns which, as we have seen, have from Peruzzi onwards always played a key role in reconstructions of the external appearance of the mausoleum; however, even here, a number of the thinner columns could well come from aedicules or rooms within the building. Nevertheless, there does seem to be sufficient support for the claim that a number of the various Corinthian capitals came from the three-opening portal that stood in front of the mausoleum. And certainly matters are no easier when it comes to reconstructing the sculptural decoration of the building—after, that is, one has cleared the field of all those statues which adorned the various imperial gardens in the area. Procopius, for example, refers to sculptural groups of figures and horses standing at the corners of the platform formed by the square base; however, while the *Mirabilia* describes these as made of gilded bronze, what have come to light are marble fragments of manes and horse tails. Just as in the monuments of Asia, the various summit points and—more certainly—the attic storey of the mausoleum must have been decorated with (rows?) of statues. This is confirmed not only by written sources—in his account of the Goths' siege of the city (537 AD), Procopius says that the Romans crowded within the stout walls of the monument used the numerous surviving statues as missiles—but also by the discovery of various colossal fragments in the area; the most noble and refined of these are the heads that can now be seen in the Boniface IX Ambulatory, whose accentuated features can be explained by the fact that they were intended to be seen from below and at a distance.

Another piece that must have fallen from the upper parts of the structure is the fragment of a more-than-life-size statue of a male figure in a toga, now at the garden entrance to the monument, the very place were it was found during 1934 restoration work on the mausoleum. Other excavation work in the Castle moat unearthed a helmeted head of Athena (now in the Vatican Museum); more than one metre in height, this is in pentelic marble and clearly inspired by the work of Praxiteles. The fact that it dates from the period of Hadrian makes it almost certain that it comes from the mausoleum. As for the two *peplophoroi* (wears of the peplum) that can now be seen in the Museo Nazionale Romano, these are copies from the time of Severus; austerely religious as well as decorative, these two female figures could have stood as guardians at the entrance to the burial *cella*. The few surviving pieces give us only a slight idea of the wealth of decoration in the original mausoleum, which as we have seen, was made up not only of copies but also original works. Together with the wide variety of minor objects used in the tomb, they bear witness to the inventivness, emotive power and openness to outside inspiration which were such typical features of the arts in the period of Hadrian. (*N. G.*)

One of the gilt bronze
peacocks that stood at
the entrance to Hadrian's
Mausoleum. Chiaramonti
Museum, New Wing,
Vatican City.

Carlo Fontana, *Drawings*,
which show the state
of the lid of the sarcophagus
both before and after
its transformation
into a baptismal fount.

In the Early Christian and Medieval period the sculptural masterpieces of the mausoleum were given a new symbolic reading, and thence became the object of more antiquarian study (mention has already been made of the large bust of Hadrian and the Head of Athena which found their way into the Vatican collections). However, in spite of the claims made by certain scholars, there is no certain evidence which confirms that the four bronzes horses of St. Mark's Basilica had originally been part of Hadrian's Mausoleum and were only later taken to Constantinople, from where they were ultimately removed to Venice. All that is certain is that the Roman numerals inscribed under the hooves of two of them do seem to be part of some property inventory undertaken by the Roman state. Two pieces which we definitely know to have come from the original mausoleum are the gilded bronze peacocks that stood, one in front of the other, on pilasters at the entrance to the monument. Slightly larger than life size (44 cm high × 152 cm long), these would later be used to decorate the monumental ablutionary fount for pilgrims which Constantine—or his sons—had erected in the centre of the atrium (the so-called "Paradise") of St. Peter's Basilica. The *Mirabilia*, a mid-twelfth-century guide to Rome, states that these works once adorned the tomb of Hadrian—a fact that would seem to be confirmed by the multiple symbolic significance of the animal. In the Classical world, the peacock was an animal sacred to Hera, who was said to have impressed on its tail the eyes of her faithful servant Argos after he had been killed by Hermes, and thus might well have stood as guardian to the sacred enclosure of the mausoleum. In a recent reading of Artemidoros of Lydia's *Interpretation of Dreams*, Alberto Manodori makes the curious proposal that the peacock could be a dream-symbol for a lover of art and beauty, and therefore its presence here would be in keeping with Hadrian's desire to be remembered as an aesthete. But, primarily, peacocks were the emblem of the emperor's own family, the *Aelia*, given that they were sun birds not only because of the "eyes" on their tails but also because when they fanned out those magnificent feathers they recalled the sun as it appeared full and round over the horizon every morning. The animal therefore became an image of human faith in rebirth, and a symbol of immortality, a pledge of that victory over the underworld which, for the Romans, was guaranteed by the deification of the emperor after his death. And it was as a symbol of immortal life that the peacock would become part of Early Christian iconography, appearing in many funeral monuments in St. Peter's basilica, where Hadrian's two peacocks once stood alongside the large bronze cone that now gives its name to a Vatican courtyard. It was the humanist Flaminio Vacca who claimed that the cone also came from the mausoleum—may even have crowned its very peak; but his reconstruction of the monument has proved to be unfounded. It is more probable that this bizarre sculpture came from Campo Marzio, in the district of Rome which in the Middle Ages was actually known as "La Pigna" [the pine cone]. A more reliable medieval tradition concerns the fate of the sarcophagus in porphyry, a red marble whose use was reserved solely to the imperial family (its colour was said to symbolise the flames of the sun). This large "basin," which is supposed to have contained the mortal ashes of Hadrian whilst his soul wandered forlorn and bereft of his usual pastimes and delights, was apparently first moved to the square before St. John Lateran and then used to hold the earthly remains of Pope Innocence II; damaged in the terrible fire of 1308, it would later be broken up and lost during the re-building work commissioned by Sextus V. As for the lid to the sarcophagus, this was first used (upside down) for the tomb of Otto II in 983, and then stood in the atrium of the Vatican Basilica, where in 1698 Carlo Fontana would convert it for use as a baptismal fount. (*N.G.*)

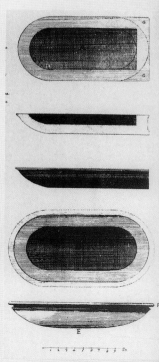

As has been mentioned above, with the passage of time—and a radical change in both the social and political order—Hadrian's Mausoleum was no longer used as a sepulchre. And this change in function was accompanied by extensive changes in form.

The deposition of the last Emperor of the West in 476 AD deprived Rome of any sort of central authority. The result was chaos, with the city at the mercy of various local factions and of the different armies that were contending for control of the Italian peninsula. It was in this context of war and lawlessness that the Christian Church began to emerge as a social authority and power; though the tragic period of persecutions had only recently come to an end, the Church, with some difficulty, managed to make a stand against the unbridled chaos and thus take up the heritage of the empire as a universal power. The religious fervour and the political skill shown in these difficult years by various bishops meant that certain basilicas became the basis upon which the prestige of the future Lords of Rome was established.

However, the empire had collapsed, and no one seemed to have the strength to stem the prevailing tide of anarchy; terrorised inhabitants continued to flee the city, property was sacked and looted, and the monuments of Classical Antiquity began to fall into ruin. Built using means and techniques that were now unthinkable, these ancient monuments at this point lost their original function; they were either demolished—to provide valuable materials for use in other buildings—or else converted to be the core of the new defensive structures created around the few centres of political and religious life that still functioned within the medieval city. And it was this latter fate which befell Hadrian's Mausoleum.

Already during the third century AD, the emperor Aurelian was the first to see the military and strategic importance of the tomb and the *pons Aelius* when he incorporated them as a forward position in the system of walls he was creating around the city. That military potential would be developed even further in the centuries to come; the mausoleum and bridge became the sole bulwarks defending the district of the Vatican and its basilica, which lay outside the Aurelian city walls and on the "wrong" side of the natural defensive barrier provided by the Tiber.

And this gradual conversion from mausoleum to fortification naturally led to a slow but radical change in the architecture of the structure.

The first acceleration in this process came with the war of 535–53 between the Ostrogoths who had settled in Italy and the Emperor of the East, Justinian. It had by this point become clear that it was impossible to exert adequate control over the whole city and that the outcome of the conflict between the two forces would depend on who had control of the mausoleum. Henceforward the imperial tomb became nothing but a fortress, at the mercy of the various armies who occupied it: for example, Justinian's troops stripped down the precious sculptural decoration to use it as

Unknown Florentine artist, second half of sixteenth century. *Appearance of St. Michael the Archangel to Pope Gregory the Great,* oil on canvas. Museo Nazionale di Castel Sant'Angelo (photo A. De Luca).

The Borgo Fire

In 847 a terrible fire had ravaged through Borgo, spreading so far it almost reached St. Peter's, which according to legend was only saved when Leo IV blessed and thus tamed the flames; this is the episode that is depicted in one of the Raphael frescoes in the Vatican (1517), which were commissioned by a pope who bore the same name as the miracle-worker, Leo X. Writing in 1614, Giovan Pietro Bellori gives this description of that painting: "The fire in the Borgo Vecchio of Rome burned so high that the flames, fanned by the unhindered wind, drew close to the Vatican basilica, where St. Leo, running to meet the danger, from the loggia of the palace made the Sign of the Cross over the fire and miraculously extinguished it. Raphael imagines this formidable spectacle, showing the voracity of the fire, the clamour, the flight and men and women hurrying to the temple, and the prompt assistance of others, carrying water and pouring it on the fire to put it out..." (L.B.)

Raphael
The Borgo Fire, 1517, fresco.
Vatican Museum,
The Raphael Stanze,
Vatican City.

missiles, whilst a few years later, in 547, Totila, king of the Ostrogoths, had an entire walled suburb built here to house the troops who were to defend the area. The site he chose, looking towards the Basilica of St. Peter's, was given the German name *Burg*, the source of the present name for the district, Borgo.

Totila's scheme was so successful that it was revived and extended during the period of Charlemagne. This political bond between the Frankish monarch and the Church was sanctioned when Charlemagne was consecrated as emperor in St. Peter's by the pope himself. In December 800 AD the king arrived in the city for his coronation as "Emperor of the Romans" and pointedly took up residence alongside the Basilica, stationing his own troops in the Castle and ordering that the area fortified by the Goths be extended to include not only his own camp but also the most important church of Christendom.

The decades of relative stability under the Carolingian empire only heightened the terror felt in 846 when the Saracens sacked the city. And even though the threat of invasion was scotched just a few years later in the victorious sea battle off Ostia, Pope Leo IV decided to extend the existing fortifications to embrace the entire area of the mausoleum, the Vatican and the district of Borgo.

LOTHAIR AND THE LEONINE CITADEL

The emperor Lothair financed the buidling of Leo IV's fortified citadel. What follows is an extract from the law in which Charlemagne's successor imposed a special tax to guarantee funds for the undertaking:

".... to restore that basilica and hold off the pagans. And thus, we lay down .... that all around the church of St. Peter a very stout wall be built. To this end, we desire that from all parts of our kingdom moneys be collected so that this grand undertaking, which concerns the glory of all, shall be completed with the help of all..."

~ CAPITULARIA REGUM FRANCORUM, II, 65, OCTOBER 846 ~

This was the start of the "Leonine City," which was begun in 852 and was destined to play such a decisive role in the violent struggles for control of Rome which broke out after the Carolingian dynasty came to an end. With the deposition of Charles le Gros in 887, power in Rome—as in the rest of the empire—was once more split up between various feudal families, and for centuries to come possession of "Hadrian's fortress" made it possible impose one's will on rival factions and even on the pontiff himself.

Feudal Rome. The Marriage of Marozia

The deposition of Charles le Gros in 887 brought to an end the Carolingian dynasty that had been such a precious ally to the papacy in establishing its temporal power over Rome: for centuries, dominion of the city had depended on possession of Castel Sant'Angelo, which since Charlemagne had been in the hands of the emperor, who put it at the service of his papal ally. With the collapse of Carolingian power, Rome once more fell back into violent anarchy, with bloody clashes between the feudal families who tried to establish their supremacy through control of the fortress. The popes themselves became a pawn in this power struggle, and were often forced to make humiliating concessions to the local baron who then happened to be in control of Castel Sant'Angelo. These were years of moral and political decline for the Church, which was often dragged into episodes of terrible brutality: for example, the trial of the dead pope Formoso, in the presence of his body (dug up some ten months after the pontiff had been lynched by an angry mob). Papal authority was totally undermined by the underhand intrigues which dominated life in the city. One example of these is the story of the *Senator romanorum* Theophylatus, who—along with his wife, Theodora, and his cruel daughters Marozia and Theodora II—governed Rome for about thirty years, using his possession of Castel Sant'Angelo to inflict all sorts of outrages and acts of tyranny.

The career of this ruthless family came to an end in 932, when Marozia, formerly the lover of Pope Sergius III, celebrated her third marriage within the walls of the Castle. The ceremony was held in the chapel dedicated to St. Michael the Archangel by Marozia's own illegitimate son, appointed Pope John XI after his predecessor had been murdered within the Castle by the noblewoman herself. During the marriage ceremony, another of Marozia's son, Albericus, feeling himself to have been offended by his new stepfather, stirred up the populace and local nobility in bloody revolt against the newly-weds. At the head of that uprising, Albericus put his stepfather to flight, neutralised the power of John XI and then imprisoned his mother within the Castle—inventing a new use for Hadrian's Mausoleum and also giving the city a period of relative calm, until his death in 954. In the coming centuries, control of Castel Sant'Angelo would continue to be essential in the rise to power of various baronial families—first the Crescenzi, then the Pierleoni and finally the Orsini. The building would, in fact, not come back under the full control of the papacy until 1277, when Giovanni Gaetano Orsini became Pope Nicholas III. Thereafter, it was to stand as the armed stronghold of the pontiff's temporal power. (L.B.)

It was these years of violence and poverty that saw the first mentions of the Archangel Michael's apparition on the top of the mausoleum, which was supposed to have occurred during a procession led by Pope Gregory the Great in 590 to pray for an end to an epidemic of the plague. The first written mention comes in the second half of the thirteenth century, but the transformation of the mausoleum into a place of Christian worship dates back to at least the ninth/tenth century, when there is reference to a chapel dedicated to the Archangel Michael located at the top of the building, probably in the area now occupied by the Sala della Rotonda.

MIRABILIA URBIS ROMAE
An anonymous work written around the year 1000, this is the most famous medieval
description of Rome. Of Castel Sant'Angelo, it says:
"… the memorial to the emperor Hadrian is a temple of marvellous size, all covered
in marble and adorned with various sculptures, enclosed by bronze gates decorated with
a gold bull and gold peacocks, from which were taken the two that now stand at the fount
of St. Peter's. In the four corners of the temple there were four horses in gilded bronze,
and in the middle ring stood the porphyry tomb of Hadrian, which is now at St. John
Lateran as the tomb of Pope Innocence II; its cover is in the atrium to St. Peter's above
the tomb of the Prefect; at the lower level there were bronze doors such as one can still see…"

Only in the mid-eleventh century was the Church in a position to assert its independence of feudal lords, but in doing so it provoked a reaction from the re-constituted Holy Roman Empire—and, in particular, the emperors Henry IV, Frederick Barbarossa and Frederick II of Swabia, together with the various local factions which supported them. And in this new conflict, the area of Castel Sant'Angelo would again play a leading role for over two centuries, with the fortress standing solid and majestic over a Rome in ruins, where the Forum had become pasture-land and the people, sorely tried by famine and violence, sought refuge in the basilicas or in the areas that came under the protective shadow of the remaining ancient monuments.

The full restoration of the papacy's monarchical power was not established beyond question until the 1300 Jubilee, an event which was held at the behest of Pope Boniface VIII and involved a remarkable programme of building and restoration work that attracted to the city such artists as Arnolfo di Cambio and Giotto. No doubt aware that the threat to their power was not entirely past, Boniface's successor would however create new defence structures around Castel Sant'Angelo, laying out a protected passageway from the fortress to the religious buildings of the Vatican (this was the famous "Passetto di Borgo" which during the 1527 Sack of Rome would save the pope's life).

Nevertheless, the papacy's ambitious projects continued to come up against unresolved political instability. And eventually, in 1311, Clement V would cite the excuse of civil disorders in Rome to transfer the papal court to Avignon; it would only return to Rome in 1376, under Gregory XI. But with the death of that pope, some cardinals elected an antipope, opening up a dramatic schism that would continue until 1417 and would once again plunge Rome into chaos. In 1379, popular resentment of the tyranny exerted by the commanders of Castel Sant'Angelo was such that the starving populace seized the fortress and stripped it of all its remaining adornments: columns, stucco-work, paving and marble-facing were all torn out, leaving only the bare bones of the structure. For years

DE VARIETATE FORTUNAE

Around the year 1430, the Papal Chancellor—the humanist Poggio Bracciolini—wrote a description of the ancient monuments of Rome, lamenting their sorrow state of preservation. His account confirms the devastating effects of the uprising by the city's furious population in 1379: on that occasion, the mausoleum was "…largely ransacked by the attacks of the populace (even though the dedicatory inscription over the doorway has remained intact); they would certainly have carried out their plan to destroy it entirely if the large masses of rubble they had already tumbled down had not made the rest of the building inaccessible to them…"

to come, that pile of rubble was nothing more than a quarry of valuable building material, and ultimately the growing vegetation there transformed the imperial mausoleum into a tree-covered hill.

Restoration work would begin under Boniface IX, who actually threatened that anyone found removing material would be excommunicated. Now the architectural character of the original tomb was set aside for good in favour of modern military engineering, with the end-result that Castel Sant'Angelo became a massive crenellated cylinder surmounted by a tower. At the same time, a covered passageway—now known as the Boniface IX Ambulatory—was created at the base of the central body, and the perimeter of the square basement was strengthened and equipped to withstand attack using the newly-developed cannon.

Elected pope in 1447, Nicholas V also made innovations in the Borgo district, turning it into a veritable citadel, which thus made it possible for him to transfer his residence from St. John Lateran to the more secure Vatican. In Castel Sant'Angelo he continued the work of his predecessors, and had three defensive towers built on the top of the square basement of the original structure; he did not however have a tower built on the south-west corner—what is now the site of the San Matteo Bastion—because at the time the remains of the Roman mausoleum were still extant there: an order of giant pilaster strips with a trabeation of festoons and *bucrania*. Not only did Nicholas V give the building a unified and aesthetically-pleasing external appearance, he was also the first pontiff to have a lordly apartment created for himself within the Castle, alongside which stood the chapel dedicated to St. Michael the Archangel (this probably dated from the beginning of the fifteenth century). (*L.B.*)

Having put down yet another popular uprising in 1453, the Bishops of Rome found themselves sharing the fate of all the other seignories of Renaissance Italy, each of which was struggling to establish its supremacy over the others but was incapable of doing so without taking the dangerous step of involving foreign states in the troubled internal affairs of Italy. And yet, in spite of the unrelenting political drama, the end of the fifteenth century and the whole of the sixteenth were a Golden Age for Italian courts, which vied with each other not only to obtain power but also for the services of the poets, architects, painters and sculptors whose works were an artistic celebration of the prestige of local princes. Renaissance Rome was no different: throughout the city, work began on large public buildings, magnificent aristocratic palaces and the enormous undertaking of a grandiose new basilica of St. Peter's (the latter attracting all the greatest artists of the age). Castel Sant'Angelo too was affected by this monumental renovation of the city; and though it remained essentially a fortress, it was equipped with all the luxuries and comforts of a magnificent princely residence.

In 1493–95 there was the danger that the French king might send troops into Italy and Pope Alexander VI set about improving the fortifications of his stronghold by adding the polygonal towers around the Nicholas V towers, as well as extending the fortification to cover the area outside the square basement, which was now enclosed by a moat. This Borgia pope also commissioned Antonio da Sangallo the Elder to build a magnificent tower at the end of the passage from the bridge to the fortress, restored the Passetto di Borgo covered passageway leading to the Vatican, and created a new residence within the fort (plus a front portico leading onto a hanging garden). These new rooms, together with those in Antonio da Sangallo's tower and the walls of the covered passageway, were decorated with frescoes by Pinturicchio which celebrated the history of the pope's family—works that were unfortunately destroyed in the centuries to come.

The adaptation of the fortress to meet the ideal standards of a courtly residence would continue during the following century. In 1503 Pope Julius II had the elegant loggia built on the south side of the fortress, and a few years later Leo X commissioned

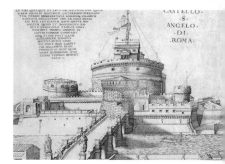

Vittore Carpaccio, *Pilgrims Met by the Pope at the Walls of Rome*, second half of fifteenth century, oil on canvas. Accademia Galleries, Venice.

Nicholas Beatrizet, *Castel Sant'Angelo*, second half of sixteenth century, engraving. Museo Nazionale di Castel Sant'Angelo.

Model of Castel Sant'Angelo at the time of Pope Alexander VI: note the tower at the end of thebridge and, on the right, the hanging garden. Museo Nazionale di Castel Sant'Angelo.

Model of Castel Sant'Angelo
at the time of Pope Urban
VIII. Museo Nazionale
di Castel Sant'Angelo.

Girolamo Dossi, *View of Castle
Sant'Angelo*, eighteenth
century, watercolour.
Museo Nazionale di Castel
Sant'Angelo.

Michelangelo to construct the marble facade for the papal chapel giving
onto the Courtyard of Honour.

However the splendid artistic rebirth of Rome at the end of the fifteenth/be-
ginning of the sixteenth century was to suffer a violent interruption in 1527
when, after defeating the French at Pavia, the troops of the Hapsburg emper-
or Charles V swept down through Italy. Rome was put to fire and sword, with
private and public buildings being destroyed, churches looted and the population massacred. Pope Clement VII only escaped with his life thanks to the
Passetto di Borgo, which enabled him to take refuge at Castel Sant'Angelo;
that structure's fame as a fortress was confirmed when it proved to be the one

THE SACK OF ROME AS RECOUNTED BY BENVENUTO CELLINI

*As the Imperial troops were ravaging the city, Benvenuto Cellini—along with other members
of the Curia and various artists of the Papal court—managed to take refuge in the Castle.
In his rather self-satisfied account of his turbulent life, this is what he says about those days
of siege: "You should know that if I had not been there the day that the Imperial forces
entered Borgo there would have been no impediment to stop anyone getting into the Castle;
and I, without receiving any award for this, hurled myself on the artillery that the
bombardiers and soldiers had abandoned, and put new heart in a companion of mine,
by name Raffaele da Montelupo, the sculptor, who was still huddled in a corner, terrified
and doing nothing. I roused him again; and he and I did such slaughter amongst the enemy
that the soldiers ran and took another route..."* BENVENUTO CELLINI, LIFE (1558–66)

building in the entire city that withstood the destructive fury of the invaders.
Elected as Pope Paul III in 1534, Alessandro Farnese inherited a city in
shock; the calm faith in the future which had been a hallmark of the first
decades of the Renaissance was gone, and the reconstruction of buildings
and public services had yet to be undertaken. The pontiff at this point
initiated a lavish plan of urban renewal with the intention of restoring
Rome's ancient splendour; and while he promoted work on the city walls
and the defences of the Borgo, he was also determined to make the
fortress into a splendid princely residence—a transformation which was
completed by the addition of regal new apartments on the attic storey,
and a new two-storey loggia looking towards Prati.

Just over twenty years later, when the city was threatened by the Turks,
Pope Pius IV would commission the Cortona-born architect Francesco
Laparelli to build the massive pentagonal walls that were designed to keep
the core of the Castle out of range of enemy cannon; and though there
was some demolition of these structures in the nineteenth century, the

outside appearance of Castel Sant'Angelo
today is largely as Laparelli left it.

Pius IV accompanied these new defensive
structures with walls intended to protect the
city against attack from the north; and the
Civitas Pia that thus grew up in the area between the Passetto and the defensive walls
overlooking *Prata Neronis* formed the core of
the present-day district of Prati.

Thereafter the fortress would remain largely
unchanged until 1628, when Urban VIII had
Alexander VI's large tower demolished—it
had begun to obstruct the flow of the Tiber—
and reinforced the polygonal bastions.

The Castel Sant'Angelo
fireworks in a 1602
engraving published
by Giovanni Orlandi.

Louis Jean Desprez,
*The Girandola at Castel
Sant'Angelo*, eighteenth
century, oil on canvas.
Bibliothèque de L'Ecole
Polithecnique, Paris.

One of the distinctive features of seventeenth- and eighteenth-century Rome was its public festivities—celebrations of civil, political or religious events that became dazzling public spectacles open to all levels of society. Wonderful propaganda opportunities for the ruling classes to celebrate themselves and mould social consensus behind their hegemony, such occasions included: important wedding feasts, papal coronations, the canonisation of saints, and the official entrance into Rome of visiting foreign dignitaries. But the celebrations might also commemorate the memory of those who enjoyed particular prestige within the city, or else be used to promote the new devotional practices introduced by the Counter-Reformation (for example, the ceremony of *Quarantore*—Forty Hours' Devotion—held during Carnival).

The best architects of the day were commissioned to turn the streets and squares of the city into fanciful sets, using ingenious stage machinery and ephemeral effects borrowed from the world of theatre. The scenography for such festivities envisaged the total transformation of the spaces of everyday life; and within these unrecognisable settings, fireworks, fountains, music and costume were used to dazzle and amaze all five senses of the spectators. Such set designs were one of the major expressions of Baroque taste in the city, a fertile terrain for experimentation with new stylistic ideas that would then be transferred to the "traditional" arts of architecture, sculpture and painting. Even the materials used in these creations—wood, plaster, wax, fire and fabric—were perfectly suited to Baroque taste because their malleability meant that they could be used to create stunning new effects and try out innovative, imaginative ideas.

Castel Sant'Angelo was one of the main points along the routes followed by processions during such festivities, and due to its position it was the perfect setting for fireworks displays. The first record of such a use of the terraces and ramparts of the Castle dates back to 1463; and during the fifteenth and sixteenth century these events were often accompanied by races (of men or animals) across the area of Borgo up to Piazza San Pietro (which in 1502 was actually used to hold a bullfight). Volleys of cannon-fire and fireworks launched from the top of the monument were also a customary part of the celebrations when a newly-elected pope made his first official entrance into the city. However, the most important pyrotechnics display was the enormous *Girandola* ["Roman Candle"] that was part of the celebration of the Feast of St Peter and Paul on 29 June. Tradition has it that this grandiose spectacle was first invented in Tuscany and then

introduced to Rome by Michelangelo at the beginning of the sixteenth century. However, whatever the truth about its origin, it soon provided one of the most striking and famous events of the Roman calendar, and fascinated the numerous foreign travellers who would witness it over the centuries. This is how the German writer Goethe described the "Roman Candle" spectacle in his *Journey to Italy*, written in the 1780s: "And the solemn feast of St. Peter and Paul finally arrived; yesterday we saw the illumination of the cupola and the fireworks at Castel Sant'Angelo. This illumination is a spectacle from the fabulous world of fairy-tales [...] The beautiful forms of the colonnade, of the church and the cupola are first seen in a burning frame of fire and—after about an hour—form one glowing mass; it is a unique and magnificent spectacle. One need only think that the immense edifice is on this occasion simply the stage-setting for what happens, and one can easily understand that nowhere else in the world could something comparable exist. The sky was clear and the moon was shining, and its glow gently nuanced the brightness of the lights; only at the end, when during the second illumination the whole thing becomes one mass of flame, does even the light of the moon appear to be quenched. Due to its location, the *Girandola* is beautiful, but it does not bear comparison with the illuminations. This evening we will go back to see the two spectacles all over again."

A few decades later, in 1845, Charles Dickens had this to say about the event: "The next night—Easter Monday—there was a great display of fireworks from the Castle of St. Angelo. We hired a room in an opposite house, and made our way to our places, in good time, through a dense mob of people choking up the square in front, and all the avenues leading to it; and so loading the bridge by which the Castle is approached that it seemed ready to sink into the rapid Tiber below. There are statues on this bridge and, among them, great vessels full of burning tow were placed, glaring strangely on the faces of the crowd, and not less strangely on the stone counterfeits above them. The show began with a tremendous discharge of cannon; and then, for half an hour, the whole Castle was one incessant sheet of fire, and labyrinth of blazing wheels of every colour, size, and speed: white rockets streamed into the sky, not by ones or twos, or scores, but hundreds at a time. The concluding burst—the *Girandola*—was like the blowing up into the air of the whole massive Castle, without smoke or dust. In half an hour afterwards, the immense concourse had dispersed..."

The last such annual "Roman Candle" display was in 1886, after which the Superintendence for Antiquities and Fine Arts asked the Rome City Council to end the traditional fireworks because they caused too much damage to the structure and to the decor of the papal apartments. The "Candle" has, however, been revived for two special occasions since then: in September 1896 and during the Jubilee Year of 2000. (*L.B.*)

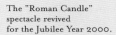

The "Roman Candle" spectacle revived for the Jubilee Year 2000.

This 1892 photograph
by Eugène Constant (City
Photographic Archives,
Rome) shows the Ponte
Sant'Angelo before the
construction of the
reinforced riverbanks and
the re-structuring of the
bridge-ends undermined
the visual impact of
Bernini's ambitious design,
whose original—typically
Baroque—intent was to
enhance this view of the city
by capturing in stone the
very flow and flux of ideas
and appearances. The
removal of the benches with
the perforated parapets at
the entrance to the bridge
eliminated a very special
viewpoint, from which it
seemed that the angels were
rising into the air out of the
water. The pedestals of the
statues of the two apostles
were also rotated, and they
now bear on the front a
papal coat-of-arms,
whereas before there was
a religious inscription,
a sort of viaticum for the
faithful as they undertook
this path of expiation. Also
note the old side entrance
to the Castle and the large
clock on the top.
This latter was still there
in the 1930s, as one can see
in a Scipione oil painting
that gives a sort of oneiric
rendition of the building.

With the passage of the time, the fortress was used more and more as a prison, and began to lose its function as the military bulwark in defence of the papal State. On the one hand, technological developments in warfare meant that substantial alteration and modernisation were required (which the decreasing resources of the papacy could not afford); and on the other, the Enlightenment meant there were increasing numbers of people who opposed the very idea of a papal monarchy (even in Rome itself movements such as the Carboneria stood in opposition to the regime, with many people ending up in the cells of Castel Sant'Angelo). Those few building projects undertaken in the Castle during the eighteenth century include the restoration of the Leo X chapel and the Farnese apartments (undertaken by Clement XI in 1721); the 1731 construction of a new apartment for the Deputy Governor of the Castle (above the Julius II loggia); and the 1752 replacement of Raffaele da Montelupo's statue of the Angel (1544) with the bronze sculpture that still stands atop the monument.

The ideological and political spilt between a conservative Church and the states of modern Europe became even wider during the second half of the eighteenth century, and turned into full rupture with the outbreak of the French Revolution. Within just a few years, Rome and the Castel Sant'Angelo would fall to the revolutionary forces (1798) and Pope Pius VI be forced into humiliating exile. At this point, the old residence-cum-fortress became a prison for those who opposed the new regime, whilst pope Pius VII was obliged to travel to Paris to crown Napoleon Bonaparte emperor.

With Bonaparte's fall, there was a further turn-around in events: the Papal States were re-established, and Castel Sant'Angelo became the prison for the members of the secret societies that opposed the restored regime. It was during these years, that the head of the Papal States engineering corps, Luigi Bavari, undertook the reconstruction work which led to the rediscovery of the ancient helicoidal ramp leading up to the mausoleum and the central burial *cella*, of which all trace had become obliterated over the previous centuries.

Bavari's archaeological studies re-awakened scholars' interest in the monument. However, military considerations still prevailed, and the full historical study and restoration of the monument would have to wait until Rome was annexed by the new-born Italian State.

After the troops of General Raffaele Cadorna captured Rome on 20 September 1870, a new phase in Roman history began: the city became the capital of a modern nation and was radically transformed to meet its new role. After some provisional measures, a wholesale new plan of urban development was drawn up, intending to stimulate private and public building-work in new areas outside the traditional city centre. At this point, two of the bastions of Castel Sant'Angelo's pentagonal walls were demolished to make way for the Lungotevere that ran alongside the Tiber; the moat and external bastions were filled in, and the structures built for Urban VIII demolished, so that the south front of the fortress now comprised the walls built for Alexander VI.

Encouraged by the material brought to light during this work, the Commander of the Castle, Mariano Borgatti, undertook a full study of the building and initiated the first restoration plans. The ancient mausoleum thus re-acquired its full dignity as a historical monument and was prepared to house what would be the core of the future Museo Nazionale di Castel Sant'Angelo. Further work was carried out in the years between the two World Wars, when the Castle was involved in the grandiose building projects planned within a city that was once more considered to be the capital of an empire. The chosen approach was to isolate the majestic Castle—as a fortified keep within its square Roman walls—from the external fortifications and the rest of the city. This plan involved the creation of public gardens in the space between the keep and the Pius IV walls, with the resultant destruction of all the structures that had been built in that area over the centuries and further loss of important historical evidence relating to the various changes the monument had undergone. (*L.B.*)

Vedutismo can be said to start around 1675, with the arrival in Rome of the Dutch artist Gaspar Van Wittel, who would settle in Italy, Italianise his name to Vanvitelli and become the father of the great architect of the Caserta palace. His "scientific" approach was the result of his background: in the Netherlands, the painting of urban landscapes was an established genre, with great attention being paid to the exact rendition of light and shadow and the faithful reproduction of the different components of the urban fabric. To achieve this exactitude, artists often used a *camera ottica*, an instrument with a lens and mirror that made it possible to observe complex urban scenes as compositions upon a flat surface.

Vanvitelli's *Views of Castel Sant'Angelo* were his first immediate successes in Rome because, in spite of a certain idealisation of the Classical, they gave the impression of

an objective, documentary fidelity and fully demonstrated the artist's skill in handling light effects, natural surroundings and life-like figures. More than any others
Views of the Tiber, his paintings were skilfully composed to highlight the imposing
mass of the Castle; and although containing numerous variations, each one of these
fascinating paintings of the monument as reflected in the waters of the Tiber—the
river sometimes shown overflowing its banks—were to become standard images of
the Grand Tour, as well as influencing the way the Castle is seen in these days of mass
tourism. Sometimes working in a miniaturistic manner, but more often in a style
that aimed to capture the flow of light in the very substance of paint, the artist himself quite deliberately returned to the subject-matter of successful works, thus sup-
plying and stimulating the growing international market for *vedute*. (*N.G.*)

Gaspar Van Wittel, *View
of the Tiber at Castel Sant'Angelo*,
tempera on parchment
mounted on panel, 20.2 ×
41.8 cm. Brachetti Peretti
Collection, Rome.
Fascinating in its detailed
account of an urban fabric
that has since been destroyed
or radically altered, this
View was taken as a model
by all the *Vedutisti* of the
eighteenth–nineteenth
century. The mass of the
Castle, surrounded by green
spaces that run down to the
river, is approached by the
bridge on which sculptures
were installed between 1669
and 1671 (detailed drawings
of these can still be seen in
the Vanvitelli collection at
Caserta). On the left bank
stands Palazzo Altoviti, from
the sixteenth-century loggia
of which the fortunate few
could enjoy the firework
displays held at Castel
Sant'Angelo right up to the
end of the nineteenth century.

following pages
Gaspar Van Wittel, *Castel
Sant'Angelo and the Apse of Sant
Giovanni dei Fiorentini*, tempera
on parchment, 24 × 44 cm,
Capitoline Gallery, Rome.
Showing Castel Sant'Angelo
from the other side—towards
the bend in the river—this
View is part of a series of
similar-sized works that can
be dated around the early
1680s. The houses of the
Fiorentini area are shown
with their riverbank terraces
alongside the ruins of
Nero's bridge. These,
together with the
foreground figures of
bathers and fishermen,
give an almost idyllic, but
by now lost, picture of daily
life at the time.

In the eighteenth and nineteenth century, Italy—and Rome in particular—became a favourite destination for the nobility of Europe. Educated in the Rationalism of the Enlightenment or the cult of the Romantics, these visitors felt all the attraction of the city's archaeological and artistic treasures, but at the same time were often appalled by the social and cultural backwardness of the city, by the continuing strength of Catholic traditions and the general neglect of the monuments of Classical Antiquity. Enlivened by personal and subjective impressions, travellers' diaries and written accounts not only give us a vivid picture of daily life in eighteenth- and nineteenth-century Rome, but also make an important contribution to understanding what Castel Sant'Angelo looked like in what were some of the least glorious decades of its history. (*L.B.*)

*"Castel Sant'Angelo, Rome's fortress, is the shapeless remains of Hadrian's superb
mausoleum. But I find it less pleasant to cast my eyes on its five bastions than to imagine
it as it stood before as a three level tower surrounded by statues and columned porticoes...
Belisario, under seige by Barbarians, sought refuge here and shattered the statues to defend
himself with blocks of marble when munitions ran out; and this perhaps is what shattered
his fortunes and led him to such a miserly death..."*
~ CHARLES DE BROSSES, LETTRES FAMILIÈRES ÉCRITES D'ITALIE EN 1739 ET 1740 ~

"Moles Hadriani, *now known by the name of Castel Sant'Angelo, was the mausoleum of the Emperor Hadrian, and formerly embellished with statues and marble pillars, of which it has been stripped to adorn some modern churches and palaces. It was converted into a fortress by Pope Boniface, and Alexander VI built a long gallery from the Vatican hither upon arches, covered on the top, through which he might retire, in case any civil commotions threatened his quiet at the Vatican... In this castle there is now a magazine of arms and ammunition, and other warlike stores; here likewise the pope's treasure is kept, and prisoners of state are confined."* ~ THOMAS NUGENT, THE GRAND TOUR (1749) ~

"*The severity with which Castel Sant'Angelo was guarded at the time of my visit (on account of the Jesuits detained) made it impossible to see the interior rooms, which I am told hold frescoes by the School of Raphael. I was permitted only to survey the arsenal, which struck me as no less cruel than mediocre. It is reputed to hold two thousand rifles... I saw a very small bow and curiously constructed bow once possessed by a Spaniard whose only delight was gratuitous massacre by scaling poisoned arrows into the crowds in streets and public places and at the entrances to the churches...*
The constuction of the castle followed the design of the tomb, raising it higher with a great, round tower in the form of a paté. *It is flanked by four irregular bastions, and another four true bastions surround it. One counts seventy-two cannon, some of them seventy pounders. In the courtyard and towards the placements of the arms stand pyramids of lead and stone projectiles; but the whole is in the key of ecclesiastical domination and seems hardly military at all, as it is likewise true of the troops on station. It is nothing but fickle appearance.*"
~ MARQUIS DE SADE, VOYAGE D'ITALIE (1775) ~

Joseph Wright of Derby, *Firework Display at Castel Sant'Angelo in Rome*, 1774–75, oil on canvas, 42.5 × 70.5 cm. Birmingham Museums and Art Gallery, Birmingham.

Camille Corot, *Castel Sant'Angelo*, 1826–27, oil on paper applied to canvas, 26.5 ×46.5 cm. Musée du Louvre, Paris. The picture is one of those *souvenirs d'Italie* produced by the French artists who spent long periods studying at the Academy of France in Rome.

Cannons and stone cannonballs in the Courtyard of Honour, Castel Sant'Angelo.

At the end of the nineteenth century, the rediscovery of Castel Sant'Angelo's historical value meant that the building was no longer put to its traditional military use and was saved from the demolition proposed in a number of the projects put forward for the new urban development of the capital. Instead, the first restoration work got underway, and a plan was drawn up for the conversion of the old fortress into a museum. The leading figure in all this (as recently reconstructed by, among others, Marica Mercalli and Piero Spagnesi) was undoubtedly Mariano Borgatti, who between 1884 and 1925 held various positions of responsibility in the ground-breaking early studies of the mausoleum, the initial restoration work, the setting-up of the first exhibitions within its rooms and, ultimately, the opening of the Museo Nazionale. When Borgatti was appointed as captain to the military engineering corps within the Castle in 1884, the building was suffering badly as a result of its use as both fortress and prison. For a certain period even completion demolition of the structure was considered, to make way for various development projects involving the area along the banks of the Tiber. However, at this point the Ministry of Education commissioned studies of the fortress to see whether it could be preserved as a historic monument. The person appointed to head these studies was Borgatti himself, who was not only a teacher of military engineering but also an architect and an amateur historian. Driven by a passionate interest in the Renaissance history of Castel Sant'Angelo, he undertook a series of excavations in which enthusiasm often outweighed scientific rigour; and when the Ministry later appointed him to oversee the restoration, he saw his task not as one of conservation of existing structures but the restoration of the mausoleum to its (supposed) appearance in the fifteenth and sixteenth century.

Over the centuries, the various phases of building work in Castel Sant'Angelo had been responses to the needs arising from its use as a mausoleum, fortress, princely residence or prison. Borgatti, however, intended that this stratified accumulation should give way to a simple and clearly-legible architectural whole, a magnificent statement of the "Golden Age" running from the papacy of Alexander VI to that of Paul III. To carry out a project that was so clearly didactic in intent, he demolished the additions to the Renaissance structures, arbitrarily reconstructed older sections of the building, and transferred sculpture and other artefacts to the areas in which he intended to create his Renaissance scenographies (often resorting to reproductions in the style of the period).

Intervention by the Superintendence for Antiquities and Fine Arts, which in 1904 failed to approve the building-work that had already been carried out on the San Giovanni Bastion, set stricter limits to the restoration. However, Borgatti still had a free hand in his adornment of the interiors, where he proceeded according to the criteria which would inspire the exhibitions held for the fiftieth anniversary of the unification of Italy, in 1911. On that occasion, he had transformed Castel Sant'Angelo into an atmospheric setting for the objects on display, conjuring up for the visitor his own *a priori* idea of what the ancient fortress must have been like: arbalests and cannons were recreated to adorn the bastions; the Courtyard of Honour was decorated with

the statue of the Angel—and with piles of fake cannonballs; and various "fifteenth-century" workshops were set up, with both original and reproduction artefacts. The result of Borgatti's work on the structure and decor of the Castle is still largely what one sees today, with the San Giovanni Bastion rebuilt in what was believed to be the style of the time of Alexander VI; the Courtyard of Honour adorned with various heterogeneous artefacts; and a large part of the decor of the papal apartments a mere reconstruction of an "atmosphere" obtained using artefacts of the most disparate provenance. The interiors of the guardroom at the entrance to the ramp and of the fanciful "workshops" in the San Giovanni Bastion also date from this period.

The policies followed by Borgatti is his designs for the 1911 exhibitions were also followed during the creation of the Museo Nazionale di Castel Sant'Angelo in 1925—a fact which explains both the rather particular character of this museum and the heterogeneous nature of the collection it contains. As has already been mentioned, the idea of using the fortress to house a museum was first mooted at the very start of maintenance work on the structure; and given that the military presence here was still sizeable, it had initially been planned that this should be a Museum of the Engineering Corps, for which a large number of weapons of various date and provenance were collected. Then, in 1906, it was decided that the museum should be one of Medieval and Renaissance Art, documenting the multiple aspects of life within Rome—and the monument itself—during those periods. However, for that to be made possible, the various other museums in Rome would have had to cede their own collections of "medieval art, objects and craft artefacts" at the very time when Borgatti was imposing his own "restoration" of its sixteenth-century appearance upon Castel Sant'Angelo. That project, therefore, also fell through; and the layout of the—now empty—rooms of the old fortress was not decided until the 1911 exhibitions. These offered carefully-curated displays of valuable period weaponry, ceramics, fabrics, furniture, rare musical instruments, plaster-casts of the monuments of Rome and various other objects of very different worth and provenance—all with the intention of giving the public the sense of being carried back in time to the period when these artefacts were produced. This desire to recreate historical settings suitable for full enjoyment of the various objects also led the organisers to reconstruct a seventeenth-century pharmacy, various "period" workshops and even a fifteenth-century hermitage.

In 1925 Mariano Borgatti was appointed Director of the Museo Nazionale di Castel Sant'Angelo, which—fittingly enough—the founding decree described as one of "art and military history"; and the "reconstructive" criteria applied in the museum were so widely accepted that various private collectors began to donate their own pieces to the institution. Within the logistic limits imposed by the very structure of the monument, the modern-day curators of the Castel Sant'Angelo Museum have recently undertaken a thorough reorganisation of the layout of each individual collection. This is no easy task, given that they must reconcile modern criteria of rigorous selection and efficient public display with the fact that Mariano Borgatti's more "atmospheric" organisation is itself now a historical facet of the museum to be protected. (L.B.)

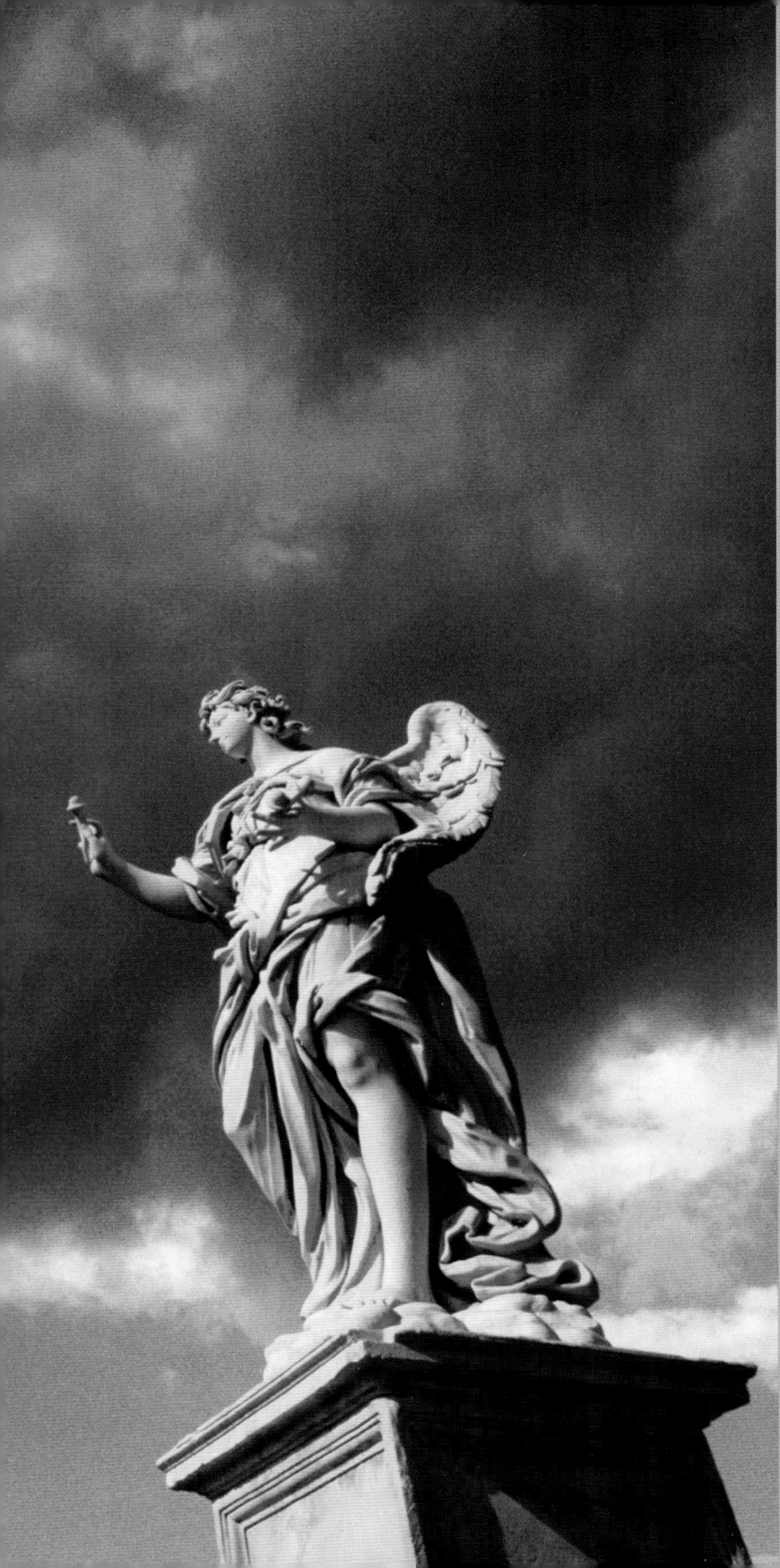

THE TOUR OF THE CASTLE

*"Just as the Romans, for the multitude / Thronging the bridge,
the year of the Jubilee / Devised a method for the folk to pass /
So that all those upon the hither side faced toward the Castle going
to St. Peter's / Whilst those beyond the barrier faced the mount."*
~ DANTE ALIGHIERI, INFERNO, XVIII, 28–33 ~

preceding pages
Girolamo Lucenti,
Angel with Nails,
Sant'Angelo bridge
(photo Z. Colantoni).

The imposing mass of
Castel Sant'Angelo marks
the culmination of a
spectacular view across the
Ponte Sant'Angelo, with
its statues of St. Peter
and St. Paul and its ranks
of Bernini-designed angels.
A veritable open-air
exhibition of striking
Baroque sculpture.

this page
Giulio Romano, *The Allocution
of Constantine*, 1520–24
(detail). Vatican Palace,
Room of Constantine,
Vatican City. In the
background, Hadrian's
Mausoleum is for the first
time depicted forming a
single architectural whole
with the *Pons Aelius*, as it was
originally intended to do;
the appearance of the bridge
is something like it must
have been in Classical
Antiquity. On the opposite
bank, one can see the
monuments in Campo
Marzio, which include the
Augustan mausoleum.
These archaeological
reconstructions also appear
in the *Plan of Ancient Rome*
drawn up by Pirro Ligorio
in 1561, which shows the
parapets of the bridge
adorned with statues and
trophies—a motif that will be
"christianised" by Bernini.

Our tour starts at the Ponte
Sant'Angelo, a bridge which within
the urban fabric of the city has
always formed a single whole
with the Castle. In spite of the
existence just slightly downstream
of the *Pons Neronianus*, Hadrian
had the architect Demetrian design
this bridge specially, so as to create
a triumphal approach from the
city to his mausoleum. The bridge
also served to link the monumental
tomb to the *ustrinum* (funeral
enclosure) where the imperial
couple were cremated; and
in the years to come it would see
the passage of numerous imperial
corteges. There was also a felt need
for a new link between the Campo
Marzio and the sparsely-inhabited
area of the *Ager Vaticanus,* which was
intended to become the site of
urban development centring
around the mausoleum itself.
Known as the *Pons Aelius* from
the name of the emperor's

family, the bridge was opened
in 134 AD, as one can see from
the inscriptions that were repeated
at either end (they were copied
down by an unknown antiquarian
of Einsiedeln during a visit
to Medieval Rome). Approached
via a ramp, the bridge had parapets
adorned with eight marble
columns bearing statues—a feature
clearly represented on the back of
a bronze medallion of the period.
Originally it spanned eight arches
of large travertine blocks which
were left unfaced in the intrados;
only the large central three of these
still exist. The end ramp leading
towards the city descended over
three arches of decreasing size,
whilst the ramp leading directly
into the mausoleum rested on two;
these latter were unearthed during
work on the river embankments in
1892, but were then disgracefully
demolished to make way for the
new road running alongside the

J.B. Fischer von Erlach, *The Pons Aelius and Hadrian's Monument*, 1712, engraving. Taken from *Historische Architektur*, Vienna 1721.

Inscriptionless back of a bronze medallion of Hadrian showing the *Pons Aelius*. Museo Correr, Venice.

View from the Tiber of the central arches of the Ponte Sant'Angelo, in which one can still see the technique used in building the original.

Tiber. However, beams and iron end-tips from the foundation piles can now be seen in the Castle Museum (together with part of the travertine pilaster at the end of the parapet). Throughout Medieval and Modern times, the bridge was the sole point of access to the St. Peter's Basilica, and thus a constant source of "traffic" problems. From an image used in Dante's *Divine Comedy* we know that even during the 1300 Jubilee pedestrian traffic across the Ponte Sant'Angelo was so heavy that the people moving back and forth had to keep to "lanes." Nevertheless, this division of traffic was not always enough to prevent accidents, the worst of which occurred during the Jubilee of 1450: a mule belonging to Cardinal Barbo was carrying two female pilgrims across the bridge when it became nervy due to the crush of the crowds and started to kick out furiously, causing panic which resulted in the collapse of the bridge's parapets and hundreds of deaths. Still, it was not all the mule's fault: a key role in this structural failure must have been played by the parlous state of the bridge, about which Leon Battista Alberti had already expressed concern. As a result of the tragedy, Pope Nicholas V (1447–1455) had two commemorative chapels built at the left-bank entrance to the bridge—according to Vasari, the bridge itself was also roofed over—and widened the approach to the access ramp, where five roads converged. The result was the creation of Piazza del Ponte, which improved the flow of pilgrims onto and off the bridge. For many centuries, this piazza—together with the bridge and fortress—were used as the site of public executions and for the display of the bodies of executed criminals (a gesture that it was hoped would curb the corruption and violence which then prevailed in Rome).

In his treatise on architecture *De Re Aedificatoria* (X,10), probably written between 1447-1452, Leon Battista Alberti shows concern over the state of the bridge and the erosion caused by the Tiber: "I would dare to say that Hadrian's bridge is the most solid of the structures man has ever built; however the river floodwaters have reduced it to such a state that I doubt it will survive much longer. With the tree trunks and branches that they carry in from the countryside, these floodwaters worsen the condition of the piers year after year, obstructing a large part of the openings under the structure. This means that the waters become concentrated and form whirlpools that smash against the heads of the piers, putting the whole bridge in danger." (*N.G.*)

In 1534 the two chapels on the left bank built by Nicholas V were demolished—they had served as perfect cover for the harquebusiers besieging the Castle during the 1527 Sack of Rome—and Pope Clement VII had two large statues of the patron saints of the city raised in their place. That of *St. Peter* is by Lorenzo Lotti, known as Lorenzetto, whilst that of *St. Paul* was sculpted in 1463–64 by Paolo Romano (it was moved here from its place by the Benediction Loggia in the Basilica). One cannot argue with Vasari's judgement that this masterpiece of fifteenth-century sculpture is of a far superior quality to its companion: the handling of the rich drapery, the tense energy in the hands and the meditative expression of the face, all give the figure of St. Paul a dignity and composure which are a perfect reflection of that classical equilibrium of taste characteristic of the time of Pope Pius II, a pope who dreamt of restoring the grandeur of Classical Rome. However, in 1668 Pope Clement IX commissioned from his long-time friend Gian Lorenzo Bernini work that would transform the very appearance of the bridge, creating a highly symbolic and spectacular point of transfer from the secular city to the holy city of the Vatican; to use the words of Maria Grazia D'Amelio, the end-result was a sort of "angel-guarded approach to Paradise." Having demolished a few houses standing alongside the river—in order to make the whole of the bridge immediately visible—the artist then designed for the balustrade ten statues of *Angels Bearing the Symbols of the Passion*. These were to form a sort of monumental *Via Crucis* leading up to the seat of apostolic power, culminating in the triumph of angels around the Basilica itself. Bernini was, in fact, taking up an idea that had already been used in 1536, when all the various areas of Rome through which the emperor Charles V was to pass had been decorated accordingly. However, on that occasion, lack of time and funds had meant that mere "sets" could be created, which were subsequently dismantled. Alongside the various arches, gateways and columns raised for that event, there were the large plaster statues of the Evangelists and Patriarchs raised on Ponte Sant'Angelo itself. The seventeenth-century artist wanted to now re-create that effect, but in much less ephemeral materials: Carrara marble for the statues

The old access ramp to the bridge, unearthed with the original Roman paving during the work to systematize the river bed and banks in 1892. Photo by Gustavo Lucchetti, City Photographic Archives, Rome.

The paving of Hadrian's
bridge, unearthed during
work on the river banks
in 1892. City Photographic
Archives, Rome.

(there are extant drawings with the technical specifications of the blocks to be purchased); ordinary marble for their plinths; and travertine and iron for the ethereal parapets on which they were to stand. Continuing up to 1671, the work involved the most gifted assistants in Bernini's studio, which had already ten years earlier cast a series of small silver figures of Angels Bearing the Instruments of the Passion which had served to adorn the table at the banquet the pope had offered for Christine of Sweden. The artist now handled the theme on a scale befitting the surrounding urban fabric, making the statues double life-size. He himself designed the models and

closely followed the production of each individual figure: *The Angel with the Column* (Antonio Raggi); *Angel with Whips* (Lazzaro Morelli); *Angel with Crown of Thorns* (Paolo Nardini); *Angel with Vernicle* (Cosimo Fancelli); *Angel with Robes and Dice* (Paolo Naldini); *Angel with Nails* (Girolamo Lucenti); *Angel with Cross* (Ercole Ferrata); *Angel with INRI Superscription* (Gian Lorenzo Bernini and Giulio Cartari); *Angel with Sponge* (Antonio Giorgetti); *Angel with Lance* (Domenico Guidi). The actual installation of the works became one of those crowded events of street theatre so common in seventeenth-century Rome, though in later years some of them would be replaced with copies: the *Angel with INRI Superscription* and *Angel with Crown of Thorns* have since 1729 stood at the apse of the Roman church of Sant'Andrea delle Fratte. Comparison with the series of drawings and clay models Bernini made in preparing the figures for the bridge shows that these two statues are largely his own work, and the pope was so struck by their splendour he wanted them to stand in his own residence (where they would be protected from the elements); hence it became necessary to make copies to stand on the bridge itself. And given that the whole project involved an idea of increasing movement, starting from the— comparatively static—statues of the patron saints of Rome which already stood at the left-bank end of the bridge, it was inevitable that the whole design should have a very theatrical culmination in the statue of St. Michael the Archangel, now raised on its plinth so that it stood free of the imposing mass of the Castle, at the tip of a triangular perspective pointing heavenwards. In all senses, this combination of sculpture, architecture and town-planning was quintessentially Baroque, because "the dramatic impression created by the Angels is heightened by the very wind that blows through their robes as it rises off the waters of the river, and by the chiastic order of the statues, thanks to which the spectator is caught up in this dynamic composition of limbs and body. Alongside the difficulty of combining the static equilibrium of the statues with an exaggeratedly plastic handling of body and drapery, there was also the complexity of a work which, unlike all the artist's other public creations (think, for example, of the equestrian Constantine on the Scala Regia in the Vatican), is not designed to be seen from one specific viewpoint

J. Zucchi, *The Procession of Pope Gregory I* (detail). Though clearly Counter-Reformation in inspiration and including obviously temporary sixteenth-century additions, the painting still shows the bridge as it was in the fifteenth century, with the two small chapels at the end.

Pierre Paul Sevin, *Papal Banquet*, c. 1668, drawing. Nationalmuseum, Stockholm.

M.Wolgemuth, W. Pleydenwurff, *Rome*, from *Liber Chronicarum*, published by H. Schedel in Nuremberg in 1493. The Vatican and the hill of the Belvedere seem to hang over Castel Sant'Angelo and its bridge.

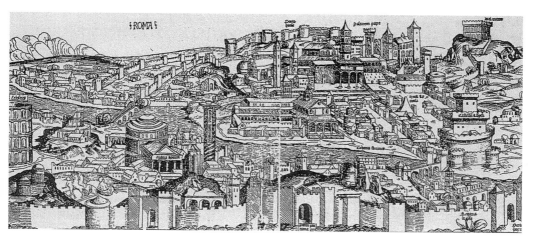

G.S. Peruzzi, *Ponte Sant'Angelo in the Second Half of the Fifteenth Century*, copy of a sketch by Antonio Averlino, known as il Filarete, c. 1462.

Photograph by Giuseppe Felici of the bridge during work in 1892. Just down river is the temporary metal bridge used before the completion of Ponte Vittorio Emanuele.

but can be approached from any direction along the river bank" (M.G. D'Amelio). This latter fact explains the unusual care taken in the execution of the parts that are not immediately visible.
As Maria Grazia D'Amelio correctly points out, in producing his bridge Bernini could measure his designs against the three Vitruvian considerations of *utilitas, firmitas* and *venustas* [utility, solidity and beauty]. And along with the embellishment work, he also took measures to improve foot and carriage traffic across the bridge, solving problems that had existed for centuries. By making the parapets thinner and shifting them outside the overhang of the bridge, he could widen the road so that there were two lanes for the

magnificent six-horse carriages of Baroque Rome to travel in both directions. Furthermore, these new, widened parapets were made of almond-motif wrought iron grills bound together by gilded bronze bands, and the resulting transparency for the first time included within the bridge the changing light effects due to the river waters running beneath it. And as the weight of the statues— each angel raised on a nimbus of stone—served to consolidate the vertical thrust of the piers, once again utility, solidity and beauty went hand in hand. Bernini had already strengthened the entire structure of the bridge, whose parlous state had a few years earlier given rise to talk of rebuilding the whole thing, with wider arches to accommodate the fast-flowing waters of the river in spate—already only four of the seven arches which had lasted into the fifteenth century survived—or even of demolishing the structure altogether. However, the original layout of bridge and riverbank access was radically undermined by the reconstruction work along the Tiber in 1892–93, when the river bed was widened to one hundred metres, with some of the outer bastions of the fortress being demolished. This work was designed to protect the bridge river spates, given that the narrow arches functioned as dikes to concentrate the floodwaters. Nowadays the slime which continues to be deposited at this

bend in the river is due to the presence underwater of the remains of various structures—foundations, but also sizeable water channels—that were not entirely dismantled and thus serve to trap the sediment carried by the current. One undeniable effect of this hasty work on the embankments was to interrupt all possible relations between Hadrian's Mausoleum, the Tiber and the surrounding areas of the city—an city whose urban fabric is now conceived of as comprising separate, functionally distinct buildings, rather than a continuous

The Tiber and the Ponte Sant'Angelo within the urban fabric of contemporary Rome.

Giovan Battista Piranesi, *View of Pons Aelius and Hadrian's Mausoleum before the Restoration*, 1762, etching. Museo Nazionale di Castel Sant'Angelo.

James Anderson, *View of the Tiber and Ponte Sant'Angelo*, c. 1855. City Photographic Archives, Rome. In the photograph one can still see the outline of the city which picturesquely faced the riverbanks.

The statues of the bridge form a sort of "collective show" of the sculptors working in Rome at the end of the seventeenth century. Although all bear the mark of Bernini, each statue reveals the individual style of the artist who created it (photo: Z. Colantoni).

whole developing alongside the changing waters of the river (such as one sees in the fanciful compositions of Piranesi). The replacement of the destroyed end-ramps with two wide, symmetrical arches (length around 130 metres; though the depth is the original 9 metres) has radically changed the appearance of the bridge; the original, slightly humped, shape meant that the structure gradually unfolded as one approached it. However, although it no longer has any political or institutional role, this remains the most extraordinary bridge of Ancient Rome, now adorned with dazzlingly white

Baroque statuary which stands out against a backdrop comprising some of the most famous monuments of pagan and Christian Rome. A place where one can stroll and savour the air of a bygone age, the bridge can be compared with similarly iconic structures in other cities: the teeming Ponte Vecchio of Florence and the Rialto Bridge of Venice or, perhaps even more strikingly, the Charles Bridge in Prague. Yet whilst the statues lining that structure are the dark symbols of a more severe and tortured religion, the smiling, sensual angels here are the expression of a Church Triumphant. (*N.G.*)

CVIVS·PRINCIPATVS
SVPER·HVMERVM·EIVS

Ercole Ferrate, *Angel with Cross*. Ponte Sant'Angelo. The statue reveals that—along with generic citations of Classical models—there were also careful nude studies behind the creation of each figure. The pose, the movement of the limbs and head, the twisting of the torso and drapery, the fall of the hair and the expression of the face—all are in keeping with the action depicted (photo: Z. Colantoni).

Paolo Naldini
Angel with Robes and Dice (detail). Ponte Sant'Angelo (photo: Z. Colantoni).

following pages
Antonio Giorgetti, *Angel with Sponge*. Ponte Sant'Angelo. Detail of the face, with its expressive play of chiaroscuro. Made of travertine, which realistically reproduced its porous quality, the original sponge has been lost in the Tiber. (photo: Z. Colantoni).

A fascinating photograph
showing the procedures
used in cleaning the marble
surfaces: the vapourized
water spray reveals the face
of an angel hidden
under crusts of dirt
(photo: Z. Colantoni).

As we have seen, documentary and artistic sources make it possible to trace the various phases in the bridge's history, but very little is known about the measures taken to maintain and protect its sculptural decoration before the 1988 project which restored the whole structure to its ancient splendour. Old photographs reveal that the black patina which covered the surface of the stone—hampering aesthetic appreciation of the statues—was gradually removed, but probably solely due to the action of acid rain (the "black crusts" remained in the interstices and the folds of drapery).

A careful study of the state of the statues revealed the need for immediate restoration, not only for aesthetic reasons but also to guarantee the very survival of the works. In fact, although the structure has been limited to pedestrians for some time, the statues—given their very exposed position—had suffered greatly from atmospheric pollution, the effects of the queues of heavy traffic that form at the traffic lights located at one end of the bridge, and even vandalism. Where most exposed to the elements, the stone of the statues was breaking up, if not disintegrating; and surface lesions created openings for water infiltration. What is more, the corrosion of the internal bolts and pins meant that the projecting parts of the statues, originally added to create a freedom of expressive gesture that is rare in marble sculpture, were in a very parlous state. Rusting of the iron had led to discoloration, whilst the surface deposits of atmospheric particles had caused the stone surface to swell and break away. Moss too was another factor that changed the original appearance of the stone, with such biological degradation being favoured by weather conditions (light, oxygen , humidity), even if partly hindered by environmental pollution. Finally, in the badly-plastered cracks such parasitic plants as fig trees and pellitory had taken root.

Nevertheless, there were fortunately more sheltered surfaces, which had maintained their original "skin" and still bore the traces left by the working of the marble.

Preceded by long and painstaking analysis to understand the materials used and the changes it had undergone, the restoration project was drawn up by a highly-qualified team of experts and specialists in accordance with well-proven methodological criteria best suited to works of sculpture located within an urban context. After the emergency consolidation of the stone surface, the restoration involved cleaning, full consolidation of the stone, treatment of the rusted iron parts (or their removal and replacement with pins and bolts in stainless steel to prevent further decay). Harmful salts were also removed and the fragments of the marble that had become detached from the body were attached back in place; old plaster work was replaced with new and the micro-fissures in the surface filled in. After disinfestation, the marble was given a final protective coating with a renewable (and removable) agent to protect the results of the restoration as long as possible. Particular attention was paid to the choice of materials used, opting where possible for stone that was similar in nature and reacted in the same way to the elements (rain, temperature changes, etc.), so that the characteristics of these additions would not effect the ageing process or the results of inevitable decay over time. A plan of regular maintenance for the sculpture was also drawn up, to chart decay and make it possible to take any necessary preventative action—even if it was recognised that, given the impossibility

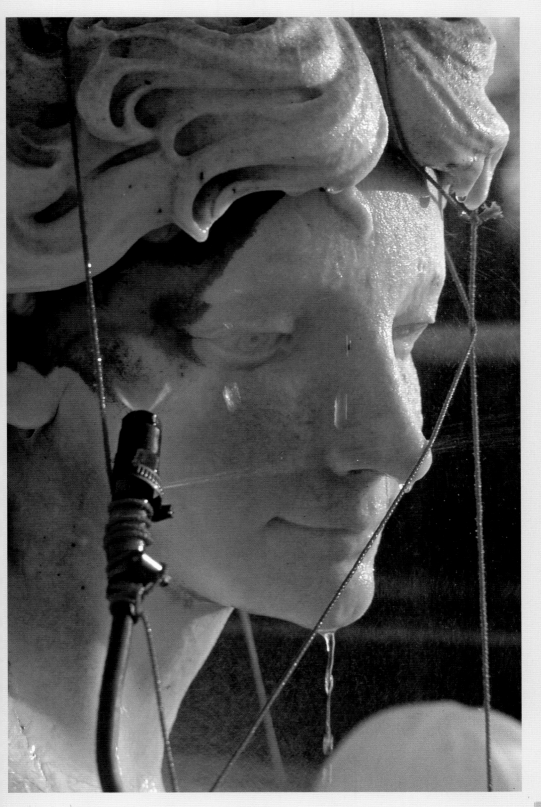

of changing external conditions, the decomposition of the original and restoration materials was a natural process inevitably accelerated by the outdoor location of the statues. The only alternative was the drastic measure which has been
taken elsewhere: the removal of the originals and their replacement with copies,
or else the erection of some sort of structure to protect them. These are clearly
to be avoided if possible because they would shatter the theatrical sweep of
Bernini's design, which embraces the urban area that forms its setting.
Organised by the Rome City Council's Superintendence for Artistic Monuments, and headed by Luisa Cardilli Alloisi and Maria Grazia Tolomeo Speranza, the restoration project was also an opportunity to study the monument in
greater depth, looking at those aspects that are often neglected in an examina-
tion of a work of art—here, in particular, the techniques used in working the
marble. It was discovered, for example, that the ten statues are not fixed in any
way to their pedestals; it is their weight alone which holds them in place, even if
ad hoc corrections were made to the bases during the installation in order to uni-
fy the final height of the figures. The tools used by the sculptors were the same
that Bernini had used on such masterpieces as *Apollo and Daphne* or the *Rape of Proserpina* in order to achieve tactile contrasts between finished and "unfinished"
surfaces. For example, in the latter, the figure of Cerberus is entirely worked using a gradine, and is in clear contrast to the polished surface of Proserpina's
body, just as in the former, the bark of the laurel tree is in strident contrast with
the still palpitating flesh of Daphne. In the Angels, the contrast does not so
much involve the flesh and drapery, as the clouds, the wings and the flowing hair
which reflects less light than the face it encloses. There is also none of the polished finish to be seen in Angels now in Sant'Andrea delle Fratte—a clear indication of Bernini's profound knowledge of the various visual effects to be
achieved by the working of marble. In fact, a polished finish here would have
made the figures so brilliant in sunlight that the eye would have been unable to
make out any detail, whilst within a closed space it has a very different effect. Just
like the schools of the Hellenistic "Baroque" period, Bernini's workshop showed
admirable technical skill in imbuing this choreogaphical composition with true
vitality; the figures of angels move and turn like natural figures within an urban
landscape that also contains the spectator. (*N.G.*)

ALEXANDER·VI·PONT·MAX
INSTAVRAVIT
AN·SAL·M CCCCLXXXXV

From the Ponte Sant'Angelo, now a pedestrian footbridge, one approaches the southern side of the Castle's square-built basement, which is nine metres high and flanked by the San Giovanni Bastion (on the right) and that of San Matteo (on the left). Stopping about halfway across the bridge one can see the remains of the pentagonal walls built for Pope Pius IV, which were demolished to make way for the riverside road built here at the end of the nineteenth century. The view from here also enables one to understand why, for centuries, the Castle was considered impregnable: beyond the crenellated walls—the merlons served to protect patrolling sentries—stands the bulk of the fortress proper, a massive, unapproachable pile that is divided into two levels and stands a total of forty-eight metres high. The lower section with its rough stone finish was part of the original imperial mausoleum, and above it—separated by a travertine band—stands the upper section faced with brick which was built from the Middle Ages onwards to house apartments and other facilities within the papal fortress. Above the monumental gateway to the structure stands the crest of Alexander VI (Rodrigo Borgia) flanked by two winged victories, carved at the end of the eighteenth century by French revolutionary troops. Taking a few steps back towards the bridge and looking up above

the corbels and the coping, one gets a view of the arcaded corridor that runs round the whole structure and of the elevation of the entire central body, crowned by the eighteenth-century statue of the Angel. That corridor is, in fact, not uniform on each side: on the eastern side (to the right as one approaches), it is part of the "Covered Walkway" built for Pius IV, who wanted a protected means of access to the papal apartments and service facilities on this level; on the western side of the drum, however, it is made up of the open walkway that was built for Alexander VII. The core block, housing the papal apartments, is made up of a long central building aligned north-south, of which one can only see the southern front from ground level; other apartments and amenities were located in a series of rooms around the outside of the drum. At this point, the walls are broken by the loggia built for Julius II, above which one can see the Angel Terrace. (L.B.) Entrance to the building is via the large gateway, which strikes one as unusually low; the paved approach was in fact raised during the work on the riverside drive. Having passed through this gateway one is in the **Saviour's Courtyard**, which takes its name from an elegant fifteenth-century marble bust of a hieratic Christ, which up until 1890 was part of the arch on the inner side of the gateway. The visit then proceeds

Bust of Christ the Saviour
The three-dimensional rendering of a image that occurs in numerous devotional paintings, this monumental masterpiece is attributed to Isaia da Pisa, who specialised in *relievo* decoration (for example, the *Madonna and Child between SS. Peter and Paul and Donors* to be seen in the Vatican Grottoes). Stylistically rather archaic, the work can probably be dated to the beginning of the second half of the fifteenth century, when Beltrame da Varese was restructuring the fortress for Nicholas V. Installed on the inner walls, the bust—whose gentle, though stylised, lines are so typical of the Tuscan sculpture of this period— would have served to mitigate the harsh external lines of one of the four bastions (each dedicated to one of the Evangelists). Temporarily transferred to the military hospital of Il Celio, the work was returned to the Castle only in 1985.

The Chapel of the Condemned, as it appeared in around 1951.

to the lower level of the building, but before going inside one can walk around the entire massive bulk of Hadrian's Mausoleum following the **Ambulatory of Boniface IX** (1389–1404), an irregular open walkway whose creation involved the destruction of the vaults of the radial *cellae* which, as we have seen, stood between the central drum and the perimetral walls and served as the base for the terrace crowning the square basement; as well has having a structural role, these *cellae* also served to protect the mausoleum against the floodwaters of the Tiber, but were ultimately used as little more than stables and storerooms. The remnants of this feature of the structure include the traces of the seven radial walls which one can see as one walks towards the

ticket office, on the right. Behind the front wall, these partially-demolished radials are now used for a temporary display of fragments of sculptural decoration dating from the Classical building and the papal fortress (crests, plaques, etc.), together with the by-now historic models that offer a very effective account of the various phases in the Castle's history and the different transformations it went through.

Niccolò Lamberti, military engineer to Boniface IX, intended that the Ambulatory— together with the outside moat— would serve to isolate the fortress and make it impregnable. Having bricked in the main entrance and installed a drawbridge, the pope would be entirely safe once he reached the Castle via the Passetto del Borgo: in fact, those who were rash enough to scale the perimeter walls would find themselves in a sort of mousetrap, an easy target for the defenders above them.

Continuing rightwards, one comes to the **Firing Squad Courtyard**, a large opening with a wellhead at one end; it was here that executions took place, to the solemn tolling of the *Campana della Misericordia* (Mercy Bell). Onto this courtyard gave the chapel known as the **Chapel of the Crucifixion** (after the painting on the altar) or the **Chapel of the Condemned** (who could here say a last prayer); this ample and atmospheric space is now occupied by the museum bookshop.

Continuing in the same direction, one passes under a modern metal cantilever roof and comes to an area where the original marble facing and sculpted decoration of the mausoleum are still visible. Fixed into the base of the drum there is a fragment of an architrave,

which must have come from the
square basement of the original
structure. In white Luna marble,
this is decorated with two
smooth bands decorated with
different mouldings; the upper
one is Ionic ovolo moulding
with astragals and fusaroles, the
lower is a trilobate *kymation* which
is typical of Lesbos and thus
exemplifies that Asian influence
to be found in other buildings
dating from the time of Hadrian
(for example, the temple of
Roma and Venus in the Vale of
the Coliseum, or the temple of
Hadrian at Ephesus). Opposite,
in the faux niches on the outer
walls of the Ambulatory, are
three marble heads which
probably came from the colossal
statues that adorned the attic
storey; making due calculations
of proportions, these must have

stood six metres high and were
perhaps among the statues which
Procopius tells us were used
as ammunition against Witigis'
Ostrogoths during the siege of
537 AD. The idealised heads are
made of solid pieces of marble
and their accentuated features
must have been due to the fact
they were intended to be seen
at some distance from below.
The first, in marble of Greek
or eastern origin, is the portrait
of a young man and reveals
an almost "Baroque" taste in the
rendition of the lineaments: the
forehead is creased with a frown;
the eyebrows are thick; the large,
heavy-lidded eyes are shown wide
open and with carefully-carved
irises; the fleshy lips are half-
open; and the abundant curly
locks falls forward over the
cheeks. In all of this, the
sculptor has used both chisel and
drill to create a strong contrast
between the rough surface of the
hair and the smooth, finished
surface of the face—revealing
a taste for chiaroscuro effects
that was a hallmark of the courtly
art of Hadrian's reign. The same
can also be seen in the second
head, which is however less
complete and has suffered
arbitrary restoration in the lower
part of the imperturbable face
(given the *tenia* holding back the
hair, this could well be a bust of

Colossal Male Bust (height
90 cm) from a statue
decorating the outside
of the mausoleum. Second
quarter of the second
century AD. Museo
Nazionale di Castel
Sant'Angelo.

Colossal Head of a Male Deity (?)
(height 116 cm), probably
part of a statue decorating
the outside of the
mausoleum. Second quarter
of the second century AD.
Museo Nazionale di Castel
Sant'Angelo.

Colossal Portrait Bust of Antinous
(total height 105 cm),
originally part of a statue
decorating the mausoleum.
Second quarter of the
second century AD.
Missing various parts
(the lower section has
been filled in with cement),
the bust is surmounted
by a right hand, making
the original composition
difficult to determine.
Not all scholars accept
the theory that it is a group
showing Death—in the
figure of the god Mithras—
striking down the young
lover of the emperor with
a dagger. Museo Nazionale
di Castel Sant'Angelo.

a deity). As for the fine third head, this reveals the gentler, warmer style that was characteristic of the Roman workshops influenced by the art of Asia Minor (and, in particular, the workshops of Aphrodisia); the melancholy concentration on the face of this beardless youth, crowned by a dense mop of curls, makes it possible to identify the work as a portrait bust of Antinous. These noble remains give one some idea of what must have been the ancient splendour of the

mausoleum, which—now stripped of its marble—still towers above one, an imposing mass built of *opus incertum* (cement mortar faced with massive blocks of tufa, peperino and travertine). As a marvel of structural engineering, this achievement is comparable solely to the lofty parapet that divides the Augustan Forum from the Suburra district in Rome or to the *scanae frons* of the Roman theatre in Orange; one can well understand how this "grey, truncated ruin"—to use the words of Cesare D'Onofrio, a real expert on the Castle—was already highly prized in ancient times. A foretaste of Piranesi's reaction to the structure can already be seen in the response of the great humanist architect Leon Battista Alberti. Commissioned by Nicholas V to work on the ambitious project of a "curial citadel"—which would ultimately be completed under other pontiffs and by other architects (primarily Antonio da Sangallo the Elder and his Lombard assistants Giacomino and Giovanni da Marcon)—Alberti envisaged the raising upon the lower remains of a smooth-finished wall of some 87,000 bricks. Thus it was he who first exploited (and refashioned) the effect created by the Roman stones, which even then hardly formed a shapeless mass; and he may even have had stone-masons working from suspended scaffolding to create the massive travertine corbels and cornice which serve to support the upper part but also to give a clear chromatic indication of the symbolic separation of two worlds: pagan Antiquity and the Christian world which built upon it in this magnificent expression of the power of the new papal state. But going back to the entrance, a modern staircase in metal leads from the large arched opening down to the original level of the mausoleum, which now lies three metres below ground level. Though we do not have a clear idea of its original appearance, this is still one of the most atmospheric spaces of the Roman world. As Tina Squadrilli has recently commented: "... stripped to its bare and severe essence, the central core of the ancient tomb now strikes us a single mass of rock, as more an expression of natural power than human skill." Wide and well-preserved, the 12-metre-long **corridor** one enters is made of precisely squared blocks of travertine laid in place without mortar, with a cornice and a rounded vault of radial ashlar. This *dromos* (corridor) is perfectly aligned with the *Pons Aelius* and leads into a square atrium with a large semicircular apse at the end wall, which must have housed a colossal statue of Hadrian; the holes one can see in the stone flooring must have served to fix the pedestal in place. Given its remarkable size, this work might not have been a free-standing statue but an acrolith; fixed to the walls, such works comprised marble sculpture

of head and limbs mounted on a wooden—or brick—framework which was then faced with drapery or armour in bronze or coloured marble. Such acroliths were traditionally used in depicting deities—and wasn't Hadrian himself a god? The head from this work is probably that one can now see in the Rotunda of the Vatican Museum. Another niche (this time, rectangular) can be seen to the

Detail of the brick wall raised over the imposing central drum of the mausoleum.

View of the massive Roman wall of the drum.

Giovan Battista Piranesi, *View of the Mausoleum of Hadrian Aelius (now called Castel Sant'Angelo), Seen from the Side Opposite the Main Facade of the Castle*, 1753, etching. Museo Nazionale di Castel Sant'Angelo.

Two vertical sections
of Castel Sant'Angelo
showing the main rooms
of the Castle
(from D'Onofrio, 1988).

1. Entrance Corridor
2. Niche for the Statue of
Hadrian in the Vestibule
3–4. Helicoidal Ramp
5. Trapdoor
6. Opening
7. Drawbridge
8. Door to the Burial
Chamber
9. Urn Chamber
10. Stepped ramp running
the diameter of the drum
11. Justice Chamber
12–13. Clement VIII Rooms
14 Apollo Room
15. Julius II Loggia
16. Sala Paolina
17. Treasury
18. Flag Room
19. Library
20. Paul III Loggia
21. Cagliostro Room
22. Column Room
23. Castle Governor's
Apartment
24. Angel Terrace

left of the vestibule, which like the
dromos—similar in its Greek-cross
layout to those one sees in
mithraea—was faced with old
yellow (Numidian?) marble; the
holes in the walls were for the
metal brackets that served to hold
the facing in place. In the centre
of the room stand two display
cases containing historical models
of the structure: one showing the
Roman ruins and the other a
possible reconstruction of the
monument. On the right begins
the gently-sloping **helicoidal
ramp** which, in one complete
circuit of the drum, brings one
up to the next floor. With a
10–11% gradient, this corridor
is three metres wide and about 6
metres high, and has a dry-stone
vault with brick centring running
along part of it; the ceiling may
once have been faced with plaster.
The floor, now of exposed *opus
signinum*, must have had a central
strip of small travertine blocks
edged with black and white
mosaic (parts of which can still be
seen in some stretches). Here too
the walls must have had a marble
facing (with bas-relief pilaster-

strips and capitals, traces
of which can still be seen);
this facing will have been up
to a height of three metres, where
the groove in the wall would have
served to fit in the cornice.
However, the brickwork itself
is of such a quality that it would
have been a shame to cover it,
with compact, non-porous walls,
neatly-lodged mortar and—at
regular intervals of 1.20 metres—
what appear to be decorative
bands of bipedal bricks (that is,
bricks that were a "double foot"
in size, 60 × 60 cm). In the vault
above are four vertical shafts in
the form of truncated pyramids.
These provided light and air,
and may also have served to
collect rain water, which was
then carried away by a gutter that
at one point is visible as it runs
under the ramp and out to the
Tiber; the bronze pipes were
destroyed during the Middle
Ages, when some segments of the
gutter were actually used as an
ossuary. It has been argued that
the openings had an important
functional role during the
building stage—for the raising

1. Helicoidal Ramp
2–3. Openings
4. Urn Chamber
5. Justice Chamber
6. Treasury
7. Flag Room
8. Layer of earth for the tree-planted tumulus
9. Oil Storeroom
10. Theatre Courtyard
11. Angel Courtyard
12. Angel Terrace

of materials from one level to the other—but it is more evocative to view them as telescopes focused on the heavens above (they are in fact aligned with the four cardinal points of the compass). The undoubtedly sombre atmosphere of this place has always served to stimulate the imagination. For example, the third light shaft one passes on the way up has in the past been identified with the terrible prison cell that fifteenth- and sixteenth-century sources refer to as the "San Marocco" or the "Sammalò"; the famous prisoners it held—who included Benvenuto Cellini—are actually commemorated in a plaque high up on the wall, and that inscription itself has since become part of the history of the monument. However, the whole misunderstanding was cleared up by D'Onofrio, who pointed out that the German Johann Burckard, Master of Ceremonies to Alexander VI, quite unequivocally states that the infamous prison was located within the burial *cella* (which we will soon visit), and it is known

to have been still there in 1825. Like the other three openings, this became blocked during the Middle Ages; and in 1395—at the time of Boniface IX—the entire ramp was filled in and closed off, the upper parts of the building then being reached by different routes.

On the right wall at the end of the passage, in fact, one can see the metal tracks of a sort of "lift" that halted here as it went from the ground floor (installed in the space to the left of the niche holding Hadrian's statue) up more than 24 metres to the Room of Apollo, stopping right outside Leo X's private chapel. As one can see from the famous portraits by Raphael, this pontiff was remarkably corpulent and would have had great difficulty in getting to the upper floors without assistance, and therefore he was often credited with the installation of the first "lift." However, various bills of payment prove that the lift as we see it was really built two centuries later, in 1734, at the behest of Pope Clement XII,

The large niche at the end of the vestibule that initially housed a colossal statue of the emperor Hadrian

The beginning of the helicoidal ramp in the vestibule. Note the travertine blocks with the holes for the brackets that held the marble facing in place.

the installation being due to the enterprise of a Deputy Governor of the Castle, who personally oversaw the (far from easy) task of drilling through the cement core of the Roman structure. In 125 metres, the ramp turns 360° and rises some 12 metres from the Atrium; here it is blocked by a massive wall—built as part of Boniface's initial plans for isolating the apartments above the Castle—and beyond that is a wooden trapdoor, another defensive measure (the wide vent above is a perfect example of the mastery of Hadrian's architects). For security reasons, this approach would remain bricked-in right up until 1890 (the pope and anyone else using the "lift" entered through a sort of passageway dug out through the wall).

Turning off the spiral ramp, from here a corridor runs the diameter of the drum—in perfect alignment with the *dromos* beneath—and leads into the large **Urn Chamber** at the centre

of the monument, which seems to have been the place where the earthly remains of the emperor were preserved. The modern approach is a ramp of very shallow steps that could be taken on horseback, which tradition has it was created for the Borgia pope Alexander VI at the very end of the fifteenth century (though the design may already have been part of the plans drawn up for Boniface IX). This alteration changes the appreciation of what was the last part of the approach to the burial chamber, where (just as on the ground floor) the original layout was similar to that of a mithraeum. However, in spite of the changes it has suffered over the centuries, the eight-metre-square burial *cella* itself still retains its austere solemnity—for all that the full grandeur of the place is undermined by the raised walkway that runs along its length (originally a drawbridge, this was built by Valadier in 1825) and the fact that it is impossible to imagine the full opulence of the original decor.

Two large air-vent windows at the sides of the barrel vault admit unintended amounts of light into the room, whose

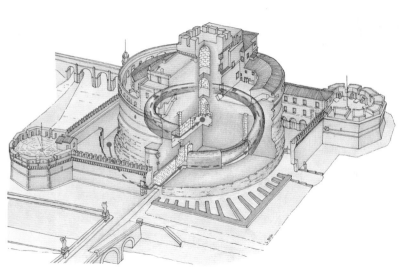

unmortared walls are made of precisely-cut blocks of travertine and contain three arched rectangular niches (two to the sides, one at the end) for the cinerary urns of Hadrian, Sabina and Helius Caesar— unless, as some scholars claim, the emperor himself was buried in the upper part of the central tower. A strip of yellow marble still attached to the north wall (opposite the entrance) reveals that the room must originally have been faced—walls and floor—with such precious materials (as a socle of perperino around the entire space shows that floor must have been slightly higher than what one sees now). The large sockets above the side *arcosolia* may have held the ends of bronze beams, from which richly-decorated lamps were probably suspended. On one marble plaque that stood opposite the sarcophagus are the lyrical words the emperor himself composed as a philosophical epitaph addressed to his own soul: *Animula vagula, blandula / Hospes comesque corporis, / Quae nunc abibis in loca / Pallidula, rigida, nudula, / Nec, ut soles, dabes iocos… /* P. AELIUS HADRIANUS, IMP

"Gentle and bewildered soul, / companion and guest of my body, / now you are about to descend / to those grey, harsh and bare spaces / where you will not have your usual amusements. / One moment yet, / let us look at the familiar riverbanks / the things that we will never see again.. / Let us try to enter death with our eyes open…"

This is the farewell sigh of a man who has lived and loved but now

The Cosmic Spiral and the Emperor's Funeral Cortege

It must have been a very atmospheric moment, when the torch-lit procession carrying the emperor's ashes (or body) proceeded slowly up the sweeping spiral ramp to the sepulchral *cella* at the centre of the mausoleum. Something of this is conveyed by ancient writers and artists, with their descriptions of solemn pomp and majesty of a cortege adorned with garlands of ribbons and flowers. As Squadrilli has pointed out, whilst Hadrian may have taken inspiration for his idea of an eternal tomb from Egypt, his actual design reflected a more Roman taste for arches and cylinders (these rounded shapes were considered the only ones suitable to reflect the unfailing rhythm of the cosmos). The emperor thus managed to associate the mass of an Egyptian tomb with the more refined aesthetics of Greece and Rome, adapting the interior of his monument to the needs of Roman ritual. Hence, he replaced the narrow corridor running into the burial chamber of the pharaohs with a wide gallery along which priests, senators, dependants and family could advance in procession to pay tribute to the deified sovereign. (N.G.)

casts a nostalgic eye back upon the desires of the past.

It is perhaps fitting that more than fifteen centuries later these subterranean corridors, these interweaving ramps apparently suspended in space, these stone reminders of destiny and the passage of time, should inspire Giovan Battista Piranesi in his visionary etchings *Carceri d'invenzione* [Imaginary Prisons], for ultimately this very *cella* itself would become a cell. However, before that there is evidence that Niccolò Lamberti fitted it out as a fortified keep: the arch in the passageway has at some point been partially bricked in with blocks of travertine, and the two square, flared openings to the sides of the main door would have been perfect for firearms being aimed outwards. The two large niches to the sides under the windows had by the early fifteenth century at the latest become the terrible *gemelle* [twins], where those condemned to death were left to starve. From the window on the left we nowadays catch a glimpse of the reassuring figure of the marble Angel; but in those days, the space under its counterpart on the right (which looks down into the Well Courtyard above the other cells in the Castle) housed the fearful dungeon known as "San Marocco," whose prisoners included Benvenuto Cellini (held there for a few days in 1539). As Cesare D'Onofrio rightly points out, along with their other sufferings, the prisoners confined here were subjected to the psychological distress of being left to die in an actual tomb.

As we have seen, in the original mausoleum access to the next level was solely by means of the helicoidal ramp around the drum—the continuation of which is now bricked off.

However, from the Middle Ages onwards, having passed beyond the Urn Chamber and up the last part of the ramp which ran across the diameter of the drum, one turned left into the full daylight of the **Court of Honour**. This route was easier for horses and pack animals bearing weapons, ammunition and supplies; and given that it was the only route open, it was necessarily fortified. In old documents, this courtyard is given as the main entrance to the papal apartments; but it was also known as the "Bell Court," because from here one could hear the bell, visible below, whose knell announced the (frequent) executions. Nowadays, however, it is universally known as the **Angel Courtyard**, given that at the beginning of the twentieth century it became the location of Raffaello da Montelupo's large marble statue of *St. Michael the Archangel*, which until 1747 had adorned the summit of the fortress but was then damaged and replaced with the bronze statue by Pietro van Verschaffelt. (*N. G.*)

Raffaello da Montelupo,
St. Michael the Archangel (detail).
Courtyard of Honour.

Raffaello da Montelupo,
St. Michael the Archangel, 1544.
Courtyard of Honour.
Carved from a Roman
column, the statue is 3.30
metres high. The copper
wings are held in place
by an iron frame. Before
the last restoration, the
Archangel held in its right
hand a raised metal sword,
with a metal sheath in his
left. Certainly dating from
an eighteenth–nineteenth-
century re-working, perhaps
with additions by Borgatti,
these have now been
removed.

After the painstaking restoration of the statue in 1987 by Gianluigi Colalucci—the head
restorer of the Sistine Chapel—it was Bruno Contardi who went against the usually dis-
missive evaluations of this work. Critics had always recognised the historical importance
of the piece, but tended to slight its stylistic qualities; as the work was obviously intended to be seen from a distance, this memorial to the miraculous appearance of St.
Michael the Archangel was treated as just some piece of urban decor rather than a veritable work of sculpture. One has to admit that it is difficult to decide what the statue
originally looked like, given the variety of restorations it has had to undergo: its position at the top of the Castle meant that the statue was not only exposed to the elements
(its wings and metal sword serving as perfect lighting-conductors), but also to the

Michelangelo and Raffaello
da Montelupo, *Leah*,
detail of the face.
San Pietro in Vincoli,
Tomb of Julius II, Rome.

Raffaello da Montelupo.
St. Michael the Archangel,
detail of the face.

Michelangelo and Raffaello
da Montelupo, *Leah*, detail
of the diadem.
San Pietro in Vincoli,
Tomb of Julius II, Rome.

Raffaello da Montelupo,
St. Michael the Archangel,
detail of the armour.

clumsiness of those who were responsible for hoisting the papal standard or organising the numerous fireworks displays held at the Castle. However, as Contardi points out, if one imagines the statue without the seventeenth/eighteenth-century additions noted by Adolfo Venturi ("the flapping skirt with its disordered and crumpled pleats" and the "swollen, stiff and out-size right hand that holds the sword"), the statue becomes much more coherent with the known work of Raffaello da Montelupo. The sculptor first came to Rome in the 1540s; he had worked alongside Michelangelo on the Sacrestia Nuova of the church of San Lorenzo in Florence, and the great artist now wanted him to be his assistant in creating the *Tomb of Julius II* in San Pietro in Vincoli. Certain comparisons with the sculpture of that monument, which Raffaello himself was to finish, reveal how much he learnt from the great master (from whom he may have inherited an original book of sketches and drawings). There are various convincing parallels between the sculpture of that tomb and the Castel Sant'Angelo statue: look, for example, at the faces of the Angel and the figure of Leah, or the two grotesque masks (one on the diadem held in the right hand of Jacob's wife, whose very melancholy is reflected in the Archangel, and the other on the Angel's armour). What is more, the handling of the hair here is very close to that in the figure of the *Madonna and Child* on the papal tomb. However, in spite of the recent restoration, the soft and gentle modelling of the Angel has been irreversibly damaged by long exposure to the elements, which has caused the iron used in the wings, sword, scabbard—and braces used in the many previous restorations—to rust and "bleed" into the marble itself. And that corrosion was made even worse in the twentieth century when, after the statue had been moved indoors for protection (it stood at the end of the ramp across the diameter of the drum), the decision was taken to move it back outside. Borgatti's intention in raising the statue on a stone plinth in the centre of the Courtyard of Honour was to provide visitors with the chance to appreciate the statue from below. However, the idea was doubly infelicitous: the viewpoint is still much too close—the figure was, after all, designed to stand on the top of the building—and its presence here disturbs the "dialogue" between one of the Tuscan sculptor's most carefully-planned architectural creations and the pure lines of the facade that Michelangelo designed for the chapel of Pope Leo X (a pontiff of whom Raffaello himself had sculpted a portrait for the church Santa Maria sopra Minerva). It was, in fact, Vasari, in his *Lives*, who first associated the *St. Michael the Archangel* with the work that the Montelupo sculptor/architect carried out for Tiberio Crispo, Governor of the Castle during the papacy of Paul III (the fleur-de-lys crest of that pope's Farnese family appears on the shoulder-straps of the Angel's armour). (*N.G.*)

Standing in front of the Angel one gets a clear idea how the papal apartments built onto the central core of the mausoleum interrupt the wide circular terrace which—perhaps right up to the Middle Ages—ran unobstructed all the way round between that core and the rim of the outer drum. The exterior of that original Roman core can still be seen in various places. On the first level above the courtyard open two large windows one above the other: the lower is that giving onto the Urn Chamber, the higher (at the back of the Angel) illuminates the Chamber of Justice. As for the three horizontal openings, we will see later that they belong to a narrow—and perhaps very ancient—corridor that runs up from the two main bodies of the building to the Sala Paolina (on the right) and the Library (on the left). Very probably the original tower was round, but acquired its present square form when it was strengthened and faced with small blocks of travertine during the work initiated under Boniface IX but not completed until around 1450 (during the papacy of Nicholas V). A coat-of-arms—still legible in spite of the chisels taken to it by French soldiers—bears witness to the fact that more than forty years later Alexander VI added the fine entablature of corbels, merlons and brick wall to complete the refacing of what was then one massive room of the original structure (more than 12 metres high), but which is now divided into the Flag Chamber and Treasury. The very summit of the structure was by then occupied not by the bronze quadriga but the marble statue of the Angel. It is possible that even as early as the year 1000 there were rooms around the base of the tower, used perhaps by ordinary soldiers rather than the authorities. However, what is certain is that the creation of apartments of a certain opulence and artistic value only started under Nicholas V. Thus began that process which would make the tower much "squatter" in appearance; as D'Onofrio comments, it no longer stood *usque ad nubes* (reaching to the clouds) out of the Roman skyline, but seemed to be solidly anchored to the ground by first sixteenth-century, then eighteenth-century accretions. From the very beginning this unfortunate transformation was criticised in—of all places—the *Liber Pontificalis*, the official registers of the papal chancellery: "It is the opinion of many that in his building work Nicholas V was excessive: in Castel Sant'Angelo he had two sumptuous residences built, one facing southwards, the other northwards; superfluous work that was far from necessary." The courtyard still bears the marks of the substantial work carried out here by Raffaele da Montelupo for Paul III (1534–1549); but even before those alterations, the public character of the space had already been defined for some decades by the delightful facade to the Leo X Chapel designed by Michelangelo.

Passing through the first doorway on the east side of the courtyard (to the left of the Angel) one comes into the residence commissioned by Clement VIII (1592–1605); an inscription above the door commemorates that pontiff, Ippolito Aldobrandini. Nowadays used mainly for temporary exhibitions—but about to be laid out as part of the permanent museum space of the Castle—these apartments begin with a room decorated with a large fresco of the Aldobrandini coat-of-arms in the centre of the ceiling and containing various pieces transferred here by Borgatti: to the left, a remarkable Barberini fireplace which comes from the Guard House at the entrance to the Castle that was demolished to make way for the construction of the road alongside the Tiber; on the opposite wall, a Renaissance doorway with diamond-point decoration. Borgatti was also responsible for the installation here of two doorways surmounted with stucco trophies and the coat-of-arms of Clement X (1670–1676), which come from the still-extant Armoury that pontiff had built alongside the San Luca Bastion. At the centre of the room an opening in the floor reveals an underground passageway, whilst the twentieth-century opening through the massive original walls no longer leads through to the Chamber of Justice next-door (home to a court whose power was mightily abused by the pontiff). One has therefore to go back out into the courtyard to gain access to the papal apartments created for Nicholas V and used by his successors (including Julius II, Leo X and Clement VII) for around a hundred years before Paul III (from 1544) decided to have built a sumptuous new set of apartments on the floor above (though even he did not neglect to embellish these rooms). The death of Raphael, the Sack of Rome and all the uncertainty resulting from the Lutheran Reformation did not stop that latter pontiff, a great patron of the arts, from trying to restore the splendours of Rome during the papacy of Leo X, when the city had been the very centre of the arts in Italy. Well aware of the propaganda value of such work, Paul III invested huge sums in schemes such as that involving the Castle, which would pay enormous political dividends. Thus, he drew on the services of Michelangelo for all his major civil and public projects; commissioned Titian to produce magnificent formal portraits; and appointed the Tuscan Perin del Vaga as court artist for the spectacular "sets" required in public celebrations. And though they have suffered damage over the centuries, the frescoes which he had painted for the Farnese Rooms within the Castle still form a sort of perfect anthology of Roman Mannerism in the first half of the sixteenth century; created over a twenty-year period, they are now an essential point of reference in understanding the figurative arts the day. (N.G.)

Groundplan of the third floor.

1. Courtyard of Honour, or Angel Courtyard.
2. Statue of *St. Michael the Archangel* by Raffaello da Montelupo.
3. Michelangelo aedicule for the Chapel of SS. Cosmas and Damian, also known as the Leo X Chapel.
4. Clement VIII Rooms
5. Apollo Room
6. Leo X Chapel
7. Clement VII Rooms
8. Justice Chamber
9. Small Leo X Courtyard
10. Clement VII Bathhouse
11. Theatre Courtyard, also known as Well Courtyard

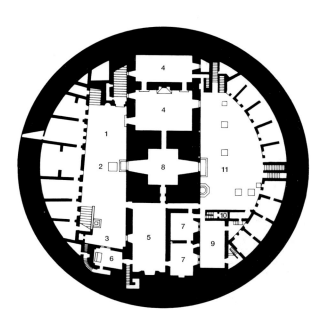

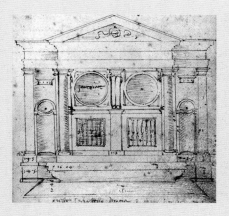

Raffaello da Montelupo.
Study for the modification
of the aedicule of the
Chapel of SS. Cosmas
and Damian in Castel
Sant'Angelo. Musée
des Beaux-Arts, Lille.

The marble aedicule which on the south side of the Courtyard of Honour encloses the large Guelph Cross window that lights one whole side of the Chapel of SS. Cosmos and Damian was designed by Michelangelo in the first years of Leo X's papacy (that pontiff's crest—the ring and three feathers—appears carved on the pediment). In a papal breve, this Medici pope refers to the Chapel—standing next to the fifteenth-century papal apartments—as a *noviter constructa*, and evidence of the work on it can also be seen inside: in the coat-of arms at the centre of the vault; in the corbels dating from the same period, and in the tiles bearing the crest of Raffaello Petrucci, who was Governor of the Castle up to 1517. The attribution to Michelangelo is borne out by the inscriptions of certain sixteenth-century drawings—for example, that in the Lille collection, which Nesselrath attributes to Raffaello da Montelupo. This shows the full elevation (slightly different in appearance to that which the aedicule had by the beginning of the twentieth century), underneath which one reads "this in the Rome Castle by the hand of Michelangelo in travertine." According to Gaudioso, the differences between the drawing and the actual structure (in marble, not travertine) are due to the extension of the papal apartments during the time of Paul III: in 1543–48, that accommodation was raised an entire floor with the building of the Sala Paolina and the so-called Library, thus sizeably altering the Courtyard of Honour, on the north side of which another monumental aedicule (this time in travertine) was built. As Bruno Contardi correctly suggests, it was perhaps Raffaello da Montelupo (in 1544 certainly at the pope's service in the Castle) who drew up plans to alter Michelangelo's aedicule to create a harmonious balance between the two sides of the Courtyard: in the end, all he did was create the niche with the Farnese lily that surmounts the pediment and contains a male bust carved by Guglielmo della Porta.

On the basis of a drawing in Florence that was incorrectly held to be original (it is, in fact, an anonymous copy of that in Lille), in the early 1900s it was decided to make some fallacious additions to the aedicule: the panels with the circular opening in the spaces above the central cross and the bench at the base of the facade. In the skilful restoration carried out by Contardi in 1988, those panels were fortunately removed, thus restoring the large opening of the window; however, removal of the bench would have damaged the marble. Although scholars have not really identified many drawings of the original design—with the exception of a few sketches apparently relating to the two-light window in the centre of the aedicule and (perhaps) its overall plan—it does seem highly probable that this is Michelangelo's first work as an architect and can be dated around 1514–16. As

Ackerman notes, this would be confirmed by the analogies between this design and that adopted a few years later (1517) in the proposal for the facade of San Lorenzo in Florence: the advanced central section surmounted by a pediment; the side niches surmounted by plaques and the large central corbel. And, as Contardi so perceptively remarked, the small columns in bronze (which are certainly original) recall those in gold that Michelangelo painted alongside the thrones of the Sibyls and Prophets in the vault on the nearby Sistine Chapel. The crest and name of the Farnese pope appear frequently on the windows of the ground and first floor, on the facade of the north side of the courtyard and (perhaps removed by French troops) even on the low doorways in the curtain wall of rooms that seals off the courtyard from the outside. Originally dating from the Middle Ages, but restructured during the Renaissance, these rooms now provide an adequate setting for the Castle's fine collection of armaments and weapons.

Aedicule of the Chapel of SS. Cosmas and Damian after the restoration in the early 1900s.

Aedicule of the Chapel of SS. Cosmas and Damian, detail of the plaque above the niche.

The stairs alongside the well were re-structured for Urban VIII (1623–1644); the bees of his Barberini family are carved on the ball of the balustrade.

In the early 1900s this courtyard was cluttered with pyramidal piles of marble cannonballs, which had been unearthed during restoration work. Fortunately, these have now been removed to the lower courtyard (known as Cannonball Courtyard), but the marble plaques still to be seen on the walls here give the calibre of that ammunition. (N.G.)

Aedicule of the Chapel
of SS. Cosmas and Damian
as it appears today.

Roman Workshop, Plate,
first half of the fifteenth
century. Museo Nazionale
di Castel Sant'Angelo.

Ceremonial plate, sixteenth
century. Museo Nazionale
di Castel Sant'Angelo.

Confectionery jars,
sixteenth century.
Museo Nazionale
di Castel Sant'Angelo.

The excavation work carried out in the Castle area since the 1880s has unearthed a large quantity of ceramics and terracotta, which has now been gathered in a collection of great historical interest. Of various periods and quality,
these comprise: fragments of pottery from the nearby Vatican necropolis, used
as building rubble during work on the Castle from the twelfth to the fifteenth
century; medieval and Renaissance ceramics; remains of the crockery used by
the troops garrisoned in the Castle; floor and wall
tiles and fixtures that decorated various parts of the
building. Other material became part of the Castle
collections after the 1911 "retrospective" exhibitions, and collectors continue to make donations.
Stored within the museum, the majolica collection is
available for study by scholars, but only rarely is it
put on display for the public. At the time of publi-
cation of this guide, plans are being drawn up for a
permanent exhibition within a few rooms of the
Castle. Hence, as a guideline to facilitate appreciation of this very heterogeneous and interesting collection, the following indicates just a few of the more
significant pieces within it.

The medieval ceramics here include jugs, travelling
flasks and plates bearing the heraldic crests of the
Colonna and Condulmer families (the latter that of
Pope Eugenius IV). This habit of decorating ceramics with crests probably served not only to underline
the prestige of a particular family but also to adver-
tise the wares of a particular kiln when they were put
on sale at local markets. The pharmacy jars date
from later—probably the sixteenth century—and
those bearing a medallion with the angel Gabriel
re-sheathing his sword would seem to have come
from the Castle's own supply. The ceremonial dish-
es from Deruta, the jugs from Faenza and the vases
from Palermo would all seem to be of around the
same date and bear witness to the work being produced in the main centres for the production of
Renaissance ceramics. The more interesting exhibits, as Otto Mazzucato has pointed out, also include fragments of paving tiles dating from the pa-
pacies of Nicholas V, Leo X, Julius II and, above all,
Alexander VI. The tiles dating from the period of
the Borgia papacy are often worked in the same way
as Andalusian *azulejos*, and scholars cannot agree as
to whether they were actually produced in Spain or
by ceramicists working in Rome itself. (L.B.)

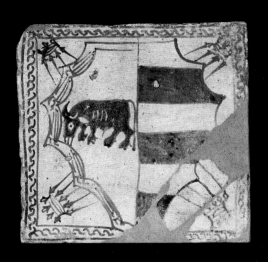

Glazed tile with the Borgia device of bull and double crown, late fifteenth–early sixteenth century. Museo Nazionale di Castel Sant'Angelo.

Glazed tile with the crossed keys surmounted by the papal *ombrello*, late fifteenth–early sixteenth century. Museo Nazionale di Castel Sant'Angelo.

Glazed tile with the Borgia device of the double crown, late fifteenth–early sixteenth century. Museo Nazionale di Castel Sant'Angelo.

The Apollo Room

Long left unadorned—the German Johannes Fichard, who was lucky enough to visit it in 1536, simply described it as a "mean" room—this was the last of those to be decorated under the Farnese pope. Refurbished in 1948, it takes its name from the series of mythological scenes involving the god which are frescoed on the vaulted ceiling. The central tondo shows two of the famous challenges that are associated with him: in the first Marsyas, having gained possess of a flute invented by Athena, dares to challenge Apollo to a musical competition. By means of a stratagem, the god wins and inflicts a savage punishment on the temerarious challenger, who is hung upside down from a tree and flayed alive. The pendant within the same tondo shows King Midas as the impartial judge of the confrontation between Apollo and Pan, shown in his usual form as a sylvan deity. The king will however rashly "cheat" Apollo of his victory, and as a punishment his ears grow in size until they are like a donkey's. Logically connected with the god were the seven Liberal Arts—depicted in lunettes—and the nine Muses, depicted in nine small temples on the walls. Commissioned from Perin del Vaga, who however died in October 1547 before he could finish the work, the frescoes were completed by his workshop headed by Domenico Zaga, who often used original drawings by his master but revealed himself to be a much less talented artist (even if one with his own clear personality). Whilst the poetics of Perin del Vaga were predicated on balance and restraint, Zaga developed the work in a very different direction. The result is that the finished frescoes do not simply offer an "echo" of the taste for "grotesque" motifs which was emerging at the time—these were the years when the decorations of the Domus Aurea were being discovered—but indulge in them wholeheartedly: the witty little mythological scenes, the putti, the volutes of leaves, crowns of flowers and garlands of fruit are all developed into an ever more sophisticated compositional framework, often loaded with esoteric meaning. The change in the decorative schema after Perin del Vaga's death was taken even further by Pellegrino Tibaldi, to whom Aliberti Gaudioso attributes the central frame of the vault "where, quite in contrast to the corresponding scenes painted by Zaga, one can see delirious processions of dancers, struggling tritons and nymphs, winged victories and demonic mascherons."

Looking down at the terracotta floor one sees various openings in it, and thanks to one of the vents one can make out where one is in respect to the route already followed through the mausoleum. The nine-metre-deep well—which seems to have once been linked up with a drain—could have been a toilet (no other trace of such a facility is to be found in the apartments) or—according to others—a trapdoor used to get rid of unwanted guests. The fireplace in the end wall bears the name of Paul III and is a noteworthy example of Roman Mannerist sculpture. The pulleys in the opening are however part of the "lift," which—as already mentioned—came to a halt right in front of the entrance to the chapel. (N.G.)

The Leo X Chapel

The papal apartments in Castel Sant'Angelo did not have their own chapel until the fifteenth

century: up to then, the popes
used the chapel dedicated
to St. Michael the Archangel
located at the summit
of the central tower, right under
the place where the angel is said
to have appeared to signal the end
of the plague. The first chapel
on the site we are about to enter
was probably built for Pope
Eugenius IV; a small oratory,
this was fully incorporated within
the apartments by Nicholas V
around 1450. That space was
subsequently totally restructured

at the behest of Leo X, who
commissioned Michelangelo
to design the splendid facade
onto the Courtyard of Honour
and commemorated his own role
in the work by having the Medici
family crest placed at the centre
of the vaulted ceiling.
The chapel can nowadays only
be viewed through a closed grille
at the entrance. It is a simple
chamber of soberly stuccoed walls
and vault, with the only note
of colour being the floor
which Mariano Borgatti

Model for the Altar of San Luigi Gonzaga

This model entered the Castle some time before 1911 and was for a long time displayed in the Chapel of the Crucifixion (or of the Condemned), as part of the so-called "armoury" of Clement X. It shows an altar within a chapel, complete with sculptural decoration, a monochrome altarpiece with the figure of a saint and a false open window in the apse. In a poor state of preservation, the model was restored by the museum in the early 1990s, when—thanks to the find of some archive documents—Bruno Contardi was able to piece together the story behind it.

The chapel of San Luigi Gonzaga in the church of the Collegio Romano was originally created as a burial chapel for an aristocratic family, having been bought by the nobleman Scipione Lancillotti when construction work on the church had just begun (in payment he set up a special fund for the Society of Jesus). Over the coming decades, disputes between the Jesuits and both the architect and Lancillotti himself led to a halt in the work, which had still not re-started when the marchese died in 1663. A new agreement between the Jesuits and his heir, Ottavio Lancillotti, was reached, but by then circumstances had changed radically: the marchese obtained the right to display the family crest within the votive chapel, but overall responsibility for it now passed into the hands of the Jesuits, who in the meantime had seen the successful completion of

the St. Ignatius altar in the Roman church of Il Gesù after a celebrated public competition which had involved the entire city and been won by Andrea Pozzo. The success enjoyed by the altar of the Gesù, which stood not only as an artistic model but also as a symbol of the lasting political and economic power of the Order created by St. Ignatius, convinced the Jesuits to commission Pozzo to work on the church of the Collegio Romano as well. However, although the public competition was now restricted to Andrea Pozzo alone, the commissioning patrons wanted a variety of designs to choose from. Once one had been

selected, the artist then created a three-dimensional model—which can probably be identified with that now in the Castle—so the patron could judge how well the finished design would work (this had been common practice since the Middle Ages).

Pozzo's Baroque taste and his background as a painter of works in which illusion plays a certain part led him to produce this model using such materials as wax and painted wood, which made it easier for him to express the fusion of real and deceptive appearances that was a characteristic feature of his designs. Having viewed the model, the patrons made suggestions

for changes, at which point the artist could then begin work on the altar itself, which was completed in 1697. (L.B.)

Andrea Pozzo, *Model for the Altar of San Luigi Gonzaga*, second half of the seventeenth century, wood and wax. Museo Nazionale di Castel Sant'Angelo.

had re-constructed "in the style of the period" on the basis of what emerged from under the eighteenth-century paving (he also added a number of decorative motifs associated with the Medici family: the lamb, the lion rampant, the five balls and the Moor's head—the latter to be seen in the ensign of the first Governor of the Castle appointed by Leo X).

The chapel was thoroughly refurbished in 1734–35 at the behest of Clement XII. On that occasion a marble altar by the Florentine Alessandro Galilei was installed, complete with a splendid sculpture of *St. Michael the Archangel* by Piero Bracci, now in the Sala della Rotonda. From old records we know that the whole composition must have had a dazzling visual impact, given that the gilded wooden sculpture was placed within a niche of "veined red marble," outlined in "ancient yellow" marble and resting on a socle of white marble. During the same refurbishment, Pier Leone Ghezzi restored the cycle of seventeenth-century frescoes dedicated to the story of St. Michael the Archangel (now lost). Further modification came in 1926, when Mariano Borgatti set about re-creating the Renaissance atmosphere that was so dear to him. The altar and Bracci's statue were removed and replaced with a marble altarpiece depicting the *Virgin and Child*; this is attributed to Raffaello da Montelupo and can still be seen here. The removal of the eighteenth-century excrescences also revealed the corbels of the original vault, decorated with the ensigns of the Medici pope and the Castle Governor.

As laid out now, the walls of the chapel are lined with sculpture of various provenance. These include the wood-and-wax model produced by father Andrea Pozzo for the altar of San Luigi Gonzaga in the Jesuit church of Sant'Ignazio al Collegio Romano; this is a particularly interesting illustration of the way seventeenth-century artists set about designing and executing their work. (*L.B.*)

On the opposite side of the Chapel one passes into the first of the **Clement VII Rooms**, named after the pontiff (1523–1534) who had them redecorated after the 1527 Sack of Rome. The identity of the patron is clear from the coat-of-arms in the centre of the wooden ceiling and the name within the scrolls held by the putti in the magnificent 1533 frieze of acanthus volutes along the walls; this latter is the work of Bartolomeo da Lucca and Matteo Crassetti, probably after designs by Giulio Romano. It was in this wing of the Castle that the pope took refuge when, in May 1527, the city fell to the troops of Charles V—among them were the infamous lansquenets (German mercenaries) renowned for their savagery—and he would remain closed up in here for six months before an agreement with the emperor was reached. In this room and the next—where the rather modest frieze bears the coat-of-arms of Pope Innocence X (1644–1655)—one can visit the first part of the Castle's Picture Gallery. (*N.G.*)

The Picture Gallery
The heterogeneous collection in the Picture Gallery, comprising works of different periods, styles and quality, is to be explained by the criteria behind the creation of the museum, which as we have seen were established not so much by the Ministry of Archaeology and Fine Arts as by the very personal notions of the first

View of the first
of the Clement VII Rooms,
with the fine transom
and mullion window
overlooking the small
courtyard.

Director, Mariano Borgatti. Given that this latter envisaged the Castle as a place that should conjure up the atmosphere of daily life in the Renaissance, he naturally laid out the rooms not only with period weapons and household artefacts but also with the paintings which served to recreate the former splendour of the papal apartments. The original collections had been split up, and so the Museum Picture Gallery was "rebuilt" thanks to donations of two valuable private collections: that of Count Mario Menotti in 1916, and of Count Alessandro Contini Bonacossi in 1928. Hence the works on display have no real relation with the building that houses them, and their distribution within it was decided on the basis of that re-creation of "period style" Borgatti was aiming for; perhaps this does not do justice to the individual works, but it provides an interesting example of the criteria applied in early-twentieth-century museums. The Picture Gallery starts in the two Clement VII Rooms, which at the time of writing are undergoing extensive restoration. The works from here are temporarily housed in the Castle Governor's Rooms, the one exception being Luca Signorelli's *Madonna and Child with Saints Peter, Paul, Bernard (?) and Stephen(?)*, which is framed within the wall and therefore cannot be moved. Drawing on the detailed analysis of the Castle Picture Gallery made by Alessandra Ghidoli Tomei. Alongside the Signorelli altarpiece usually hangs a predella with *Stories from the Life of St. John the Baptist*, probably produced by his workshop to original drawings by the master himself; in the past, it was thought to be by Signorelli's own hand and erroneously linked with the larger painting. This latter is probably the work that Signorelli painted in 1523 for the convent of San Michelangelo in Cortona, where the work remained (in the hands of private collectors) until it passed into the Florentine collection of Contini Bonacossi. For reasons of conservation transferred from its original wood panel to canvas, this oil painting shows the *Virgin in Glory with Angels and Cherubs*, together with four male saints, all seen against a landscape background. In the foreground one can recognise St. Paul (with a book and the sword that was the instrument of his martyrdom) and St. Peter (with a book and the keys); behind them, is a deacon saint with no identifying attributes (considered to be either St. Stephen or St. Vincent) and another figure who has been identified as either St. Bernard or St. Benedict

(the nuns who commissioned the work were members of a Benedictine order). Born in Cortona around 1445, Luca Signorelli trained as an artist in the Umbrian school of Piero della Francesca, the characteristic features of which were careful perspective construction of pictorial space and the solid, plastic handling of the human anatomy. However, a tortured soul, Signorelli abandoned the rational and controlled world of Della Francesca's art and moved to Florence, where the apocalyptic sermons of Gerolamo Savonarola were sparking off a profound moral and religious crisis that was beginning to undermine the serenity that had been such a characteristic of the Early Renaissance. Here the artist was fascinated by the dramatic and dynamic compositions of Pollaiolo, and thence developed his own very personal style, which finds its greatest expression in the

Luca Signorelli, *Madonna and Child with SS. Peter, Paul, Bernard (?) and Stephen(?)*, 1523, originally oil on panel, now transferred to canvas (detail). Museo Nazionale di Castel Sant'Angelo (photo A. De Luca).

frescoes of Orvieto cathedral. The *Zavattari Polyptych* is one of the most important extant expressions of the International Gothic style as it developed in the Lombardy area; indeed, according to Roberto Longhi, it is the most significant "of the small amount of Lombard material that has come down to us." Surmounted by typical Gothic arches, its seven panels depict: *The Virgin and Child Enthroned with Two Angels*, and—to the sides—*St. Anthony Abbot, A Martyr Saint, St. John the Baptist, St. Ambrose, St. Peter* and *St. Benedict*. Originally the works will have been enclosed within a carved and gilded frame that was in keeping with the rich traditions of Lombard craftsmanship; they were probably removed when the work came onto the market, with each panel being sold separately: Castel Sant'Angelo originally obtained five of the panels as a result of the Contini donation, whilst the other two—*St. Anthony Abbot* and *St. Benedict*—passed into a private collection in Rome and have only recently entered the museum. The large polyptych—the frame must have measured something like two metres wide and three metres high—was painted in the Milan area and probably, given its size and quality, was destined for an important local church: the presence of St. John the Baptist and St. Ambrose, respectively patron saints of Monza and Milan, suggests it was in one of these two cities. The artists are identified with those "masters of the bottega degli Zavattari," a highly-skilled group of painters working in the Milan area during the middle decades of the fifteenth century and known to have painted the magnificent 1444 fresco cycle of the *Life of Theodolinda* in Monza Cathedral. Just as in that work, the artists involved in creating this Castel Sant'Angelo polyptych were numerous; it was the norm in the artistic workshops of medieval Lombardy for the artists to specialize in one particular part of the composition (for example, backgrounds or faces). As Borgatti noted, the work here seems to be inspired by International Gothic, a courtly style of painting that enjoyed great vogue in the cities of the Po Valley from the end of the fourteenth century throughout the fifteenth. Characteristic features of the work, therefore, are its profusion of gold, the elegance of the figures themselves and the wealth of precious detail. All in all, the subject-matter may be religious but the atmosphere is one of fairytale opulence, as befitted the refined tastes of the patrons who commissioned such paintings. On the basis of comparisons with the Monza frescoes, scholars date these works around the 1430s. The small painting of *Christ Bearing the Cross* has kept all its intensity of expression, even if rather damaged by the loss of glaze and paint in various areas of the surface. Part of the Menotti donation to the museum, this work was attributed by Bernard Berenson to Giampietrino, a Lombard artist active in the first half of the sixteenth century and profoundly influenced by the style of Leonardo da Vinci. The latter's presence at the Milan court of Ludovico il Moro would have a great effect on local artists, who were traditionally expert in using the expressive potential of light and therefore showed particular interest in the Tuscan artist's attempts to express the "mobility of the soul"—attempts which in Milan itself would culminate in the creation of the wondrous *Last Supper*.

Giampietrino would be one of the major disciples of Leonardo in Lombardy, and this *Christ Bearing the Cross* would seem to be modelled on the Tuscan master's work. Recent restoration undertaken by the museum has brought out the full quality of the small panel painting; the soft brushstrokes and the particular gentleness in Christ's expression seem to confirm that the work may be attributed either to Giampietrino or an artist of his circle and dated around the 1540s.

Another work very close in style to that of the Lombard painter is the *Mocking of Christ*, again from the Menotti Collection, in which the grotesque caricatures used in depicting the tormentors reveal the strong influence of Northern European painting. The small panel painting of the *Circumcision of Christ* has a more lively, narrative tone, with the main characters surrounded by a crowd in sixteenth-century costume. Probably part of the predella of a polyptych, this work is attributed to Marcello Fogolino, an artist from Vicenza (c. 1483–1558). Forced to flee the Veneto following a accusation of murder, Fogolino took refuge in Trento, where he placed himself under the protection of the bishop-prince and, together with Romanino and Dosso Dossi, worked on the decoration of the Castello del Buonconsiglio. These two masters—one from Brescia, the other from Romagna (yet particularly receptive to the culture of the Veneto)—were to have a very beneficial influence on Fogolino's work, which thence showed very refined use of colour and great vivacity of expression. The panel paintings of *St. John the Baptist* and *St. Sebastian* come from the Contini Bonacossi collection and are attributed to Niccolò di Liberatore, an artist born and trained in Umbria but also highly influenced by the example of Veneto art. Known as "L'Alunno" (the Pupil), this

artist lived in Foligno from 1430 to 1502, and according to experts the panels in the Castle Museum are mature works to be dated around 1485: probably they are the two side panels to a small triptych, the central part of which—the *Assumption of the Virgin*—can now be seen in the church of Santa Maria Assunta at Alviano. The Castle Governor's Rooms also contain Cavalier D'Arpino's large *Portrait of Prospero Farinacci*. This signed work shows the Procurator Fiscal of Pope Paul V who acted as defence attorney to Beatrice Cenci during the famous trial that was held in this very Castle. Probably the painting of it was of some use to the artist himself when he had his own fiscal problems: in fact, stylistic analysis suggests the work dates from the end of the first decade of the seventeenth century, and we know that it was in 1607 that Cavalier D'Arpino suffered a distraint of all goods. (*L.B.*)

The Zavattari Workshop, *Polyptych*, 1430s, tempera on panel, detail of the panels from the Contini Bonacossi Collection. Museo Nazionale di Castel Sant'Angelo.

"The sublime captured in a line that is malleable, uneasy and often heart-rending..." Roberto Longhi

The Museo Nazionale di Castel Sant'Angelo houses two small but extremely valuable panels of *Christ of the Benediction* and *St. Honofrius*, which were painted towards the very end of his life (1494) by Carlo Crivelli. A lone artist, born in Venice c. 1430, Crivelli perhaps trained in the workshops of the Vivarini and Jacopo Bellini, but would later come within the orbit of the Padua school, sharing the Squarcione circle's enthusiasm for the anti-Classical features in Donatello's work and the incisive, analytical line of Mantegna. Ultimately he would, like the very heterodoxical Ferrara School, show himself capable of combining a pervasive taste for gilded and fanciful settings with a style that explored the full variety of human experience, sublimating the sufferings of pseudo-Renaissance man in countless works that are of consistently excellent quality.

Crivelli's departure from Venice was initially the result of a charge of adultery, and the fact that he felt piercing nostalgia for the city is revealed by his continuing to sign himself CAROLVS CRIVELLVS VENETVS. However, he could not return, and from his initial refuge in Dalmatia he moved to the Marches, where he lived and worked for more than thirty years. Much admired in a region that was nevertheless remote from the more famous centres of Renaissance art, his work would remain practically ignored for centuries to come; this was the same sort of unhappy fate that befell another Venetian who worked in the Marches—Lorenzo Lotto—who is also represented in this museum by a masterpiece. Undervalued as a result of changing tastes, Crivelli's altarpieces were removed to be replaced with works by contemporary artists which reflected the ideals of the Counter-Reformation. As a result they fell prey to sharp-eyed collectors and were gradually split up, with individual parts ending up in museums all over the world; it was not until the nineteenth century—with the Neo-Gothic revival and the advent of the Pre-Raphaelites—that the artist's critical fortunes changed.

The pieces exhibited in the second of the Clement VII Rooms are themselves the result of one of those wretched divisions of complete altarpieces. And though one can still appreciate the aesthetic value of the works, one cannot help but feel that the original cultural import of a painting is impoverished when that work is taken from the place it was intended to occupy. It was Federico Zeri's sharp eye which first identified the two Castel Sant'Angelo panels as parts of the predella of the *Coronation of the Virgin* altarpiece painted for the church of San Francesco in Fabriano and now recomposed—with the powerful *Pietà* of the cyma—in the Brera Museum, Milan. The attribution is confirmed by a notarial document from the Fabriano archives dated 9 January 1490, in which the artist accepts the commission for a work whose iconography is of clearly Franciscan inspiration: the completion of the main panel with a predella ("Dominus Carolus facere promisit scabellum dicte tabule et dipingere in eos figuras apostolo-

Reconstruction of the *Coronation of the Virgin* altarpiece, with its predella, painted by Carlo Crivelli in 1490–94 for the church of San Francesco in Fabriano. I. *The Pietà*, tempera on arched panel, 128 × 250 cm (?). Pinacoteca di Brera, Milan; II. *Coronation of the Virgin*, tempera on panel, 225 × 255 cm. Pinacoteca di Brera, Milan; III. *St. Bernardino of Siena*, tempera on panel, 28 × 25 cm, Keresztény Múzeum, Esztergom; IV. *St. Anthony of Padua*, tempera on panel, 28 × 22 cm. Keresztény Múzeum, Esztergom; V. *SS. Ludovic of Toulouse, Jerome and Peter the Apostle*, tempera on panel, 28 × 76 cm. Musée Jacquemart-André, Paris; VI. *Christ of the Benediction*, tempera on panel, 28 × 25 cm. Museo Nazionale di Castel Sant'Angelo; VII. *SS. Paul, John Chrysostom and Basil*, tempera on panel, 28 × 76 cm. Musée Jacquemart-André, Paris; VIII. *St. Dominic*, tempera on panel, 28 × 22 cm. Keresztény Múzeum, Esztergom; IX. *St. Honofrius*, tempera on panel, 28 × 25 cm. Museo Nazionale di Castel Sant'Angelo.

rum vel historiam alicuius sancti") and friezes and gilding for the "ornament and perfection" of the entire work. The whole thing was a sizeable undertaking, given that the altarpiece (for the high altar) was around five metres high and—including frame—more than three metres wide. Finished some time after the *Coronation*, which is signed and dated 1493, the *scabellum* itself must have been completed by 7 August 1494, when Crivelli declared his contract fully settled and issued the friars of Fabriano with a receipt. This is the very last we hear of the artist until the next year, when his brother, Vittore, applied to the Commune of Ascoli Piceno for possession of his estate.

In effect, this work is Crivelli's spiritual last Will and Testament. However, it was removed and sold off in the eighteenth century, when the church—which no longer exists—was rebuilt in keeping with the prevailing cultural tastes of the day. Nothing is known about the whereabouts of the various paintings after their division. It is probable that they passed through Rome, which was attracting a lot of works from the Marches in those years; yet it is clear that the predella did not follow the two main panels to Milan, but was further divided into its constituent parts—some of which went to France and some to Hungary. The only two to stay in Italy are these Roman fragments, which were ultimately bought by the Count Mario Menotti who in 1916 would donate them—and numerous other works of sixteenth- and seventeenth-century art—to the museum. One can readily agree with Zeri's claim that the *Christ of the Benediction* occupied the centre of the predella—as it does in those to another couple of polyptychs painted by Crivelli (further proof comes from the perspective used in painting the arch). To the left will have come the panels with *St. Ludovic of Toulouse*, *St. Jerome*, *St. Peter*, and to the right, *St. Paul*, *St. John Chrysostom* and *St. Basil* (these latter two are now in the Musée Jacquemart-André in Paris). That saints Peter and Paul were placed alongside Christ is proved by the traces of fruit hanging down from the columns of the loggietta housing the saints, which were painted over when the predella was split up (in order to make each part a complete, individual painting); the same over-painting has also been found in the Castel Sant'Angelo panel. Rather less certain is the claim that *St. Bernardino of Siena* and the Castel Sant'Angelo *St. Honofrius* are to be placed at the base of the frame, to the left and right respectively (the space on the inside of each being occupied by the severely-trimmed panels of St. Anthony of Padua and St. Dominic, now in the Christianus Museum in Esztergom). By offering this reconstruction, Zeri is forced to make good the shortfall in the width of the predella with the coats-of-arms of the two friars who headed the monastery at the time when the work was completed: Jacopo da Fabriano and Angelo Serra de' Conti. But who is to say that there were not other small panels of saints which we know nothing about? Nevertheless, the existence of the small panels at the base of a majestic frame resting on half-columns may however be confirmed by three facts: a) the actual contract for the installation, which mentions the magnificence of the decoration and of the painted friezes within the frame; b) the uniformly brownish colour of the niches in the spans that enclose the saints in question, compared to the clearer arcades which stand out against marmorized pendentives in the Paris panels; here, it is to be noted that the architecture of the *St. Honofrius* however has been repainted; c) by the single—and I would say, odd—piece of evidence supplied by a small panel of St. Catherine within a similar arch with a denser ashlar lintel at the base of one of the strip pilasters decorated with candlesticks that are part of the frame of the *Madonna of the Swallows* altarpiece that Crivelli painted around this time (post 1491) for another Franciscan church in nearby Matelica (now to be seen, in its complete state, at

Carlo Crivelli, *Christ of the Benediction*, tempera on panel, 28 × 25 cm. Museo Nazionale di Castel Sant'Angelo. The last of the treatments of this subject in panels of around the same size (for example, the predellae of the 1472 *Polyptych* and the *Montefiore Polyptych*, now both in American collections), the *Christ of the Benediction* rests his left hand on a book in which unfortunately we cannot read the script that confirms his divine origin. Pain and sorrow are made vivid by his stigmata; but the open mouth also seems to offer words of hope as he glances down at the faithful. The simplicity adds to the fascination of a man who seems to hover between two worlds, the terrestrial and the celestial. In this work, Crivelli's crisp and tense line seems to become less oneiric and edgy, more delicate and warm. Against the dark background of the niche, the Christ with soft golden hair that one can almost touch, stands out clearly. In effect, here he is *triumphans*, whilst in the cyma he is shown *patiens*. The piers at the sides were decorated with festoons of fruit, which were long considered to be a sort of personal mannerism of Crivelli's, but were actually used by various other artists of the period for this type of decoration. In effect, they are rich in symbols of Christ and the Virgin. In the part that has survived the breaking-up of the predella one can recognise an apple and a cucumber. The former clearly makes a reference to Eve and the Original Sin, the burden of which Christ was said to take upon himself through his incarnation. The latter is, in fact, a symbol of the resurrection thanks to one of those frequent parallels established between the Old and New Testaments: for three days Jonah remained in the whale—just as Christ was three days in Hell after his Crucifixion—and when he was vomited up by the leviathan, he found himself in the shade of a pergola of pumpkin plants. Itself another *cucurbitacea*, the cucumber too thus became a symbol of the Resurrection.

Carlo Crivelli, *St. Honofrius*, tempera on panel, 28 × 25 cm. Museo Nazionale di Castel Sant'Angelo. Over the centuries, the niche has probably been repainted several times: the paint is applied in a much more summary way than is usual in Crivelli's work, and there is too sharp a colour distinction between the side piers and the dense lintel of ashlar. Within it, Crivelli places his one rendition of the figure of St. Honofrius, the famous Egyptian hermit known to us only through legend rather than historical fact. Of royal descent, Honofrius—his name in Greek means "he who is always happy"—became fascinated by the examples set by the prophet Elijah and St. John the Baptist, who achieved the height of virtue by withdrawing into the solitude of the desert. Leaving the city of Thebes, the saint thus lived for more than sixty years a life of total asceticism and privation, to the point that he almost became a grotesque caricature of the non-human. Crivelli renders this "wild" old man perfectly, with his long hair and white beard covering nearly the whole of his body; the only clothing being a loincloth of leafs highlighted in gold. The painting of the—far from shaggy—hair and beard is particularly fine, whilst the modelling of the face and body is equally sharp and clear. Look, for example, at the powerful, dark-skinned arms and the long-nailed fingers that hold a cross and knotted stick (arranged to form a very balanced composition); the latter indeed, is not only a sign of his existence as an anchorite, but also a necessary support in his old age. In the grimace on his face, the old man seems to be exhorting each one of us to fulfil our vocations, without seeking escape in a life that is ephemeral—or, rather, that does not really belong to us. There seems to be an interrupted dialogue with the viewer, an invitation to think upon what we have heard... On the nearby hill of the Janiculum, one can read the whole history of the hermit's life in the seventeenth-century fresco cycle in the cloisters of the church, at a place that was so dear to Torquato Tasso and Chateaubriand—one can read the whole history of thehermit's life in the seventeenth-century fresco cycle within the cloisters of the church dedicated to the saint after his tardy admission to the martyrology.

the London National Gallery). If that saint had not already been depicted in the *Coronation* itself—the one female presence—one might (on the basis of the size: 29 × 21 cm) argue that it comes from the series in question, given that it is very out of keeping with the other panels in the London work, which are all narrative in content. Whatever the truth, this is a preliminary trial for a more demanding architectural composition—such as one sees in the Fabriano predella, with its continuous loggia of rustic archivolts, originally cut at the top (the preparatory studies for this have been revealed as the charcoal lines have begun to show through the ageing surface of the paint).

A late work, the Fabriano altarpiece is one in which the artist makes his greatest concessions to the prevailing tastes of the day: as had happened in the *Christ giving the Keys to St. Peter* and the above-mentioned *Madonna of the Swallows*, Crivelli abandons the closed sections of a polyptych for this Florentine-Veneto style altarpiece. The predella too must therefore have been transformed to make it in keeping with the whole work. The line of wooden arches on thin columns enclosing half-busts set against a gold background was replaced by a non-realistic stone loggietta within which the artist seems to amuse himself in capturing the saints in the most bizarre poses. These striking feats of painting add a certain liveliness, whilst the open and closed books resting on the ledge create a sense of shadow and depth that serves to set the viewer at the necessary distance. It has been said that the new unified structure for altarpieces—which was undoubtedly more congenial to such artists as Giovanni Bellini or Piero della Francesca (others artists who also worked in the Marches)—might lead to a certain weakness of overall form; and, at least as far as the *Coronation of the Virgin* is concerned, it is perhaps true that while the whole may be well-articulated, there is a certain repetitiveness in the compositional schema and a redundancy of decoration. However, the cyma certainly shows no falling-off in the artist's abilities, with purity of line used to create an atmosphere of severe elegance, in which each of the figures is lost in their own solitary grief. The interweaving of the emaciated hands of Mary Magdalene and the dead Christ is a veritable masterpiece of pictorial invention, with the hole pierced by the nail rendered with harsh realism. And then there is powerful effect of the open book and the trembling flame of the candle, almost torn from its wick. As Pietro Zampetti, the most perception and authoritative of Crivelli scholars noted: "if our attention moves from the whole to the single fragments of truth that he focused on to highlight as individual facts, then the innovations he presents us with seem to reveal his artistic personality in its entirety." In effect, Crivelli is the first to give expression to a modern "poetics of the object." The artist moves away from the Venetian painters' concern with the expression of a feeling for the natural world or the universe around them, to focus his attention on the things seen as part of everyday life. Hence, while this predella, whose attribution is beyond doubt, may be his last work, it is also his most innovative. In his more courtly works, the figures are shown with tense masks and there is a metallic harshness of drapery (which, however, reveals a sort of Flemish subtlety of technique in exalting the very opulence of precious materials), but when we come to these Castel Sant'Angelo panels we find two much humbler figures, whose features are rendered in more rapid, expressionistic strokes—and it is this which means that we are dramatically caught up in their torments and suffering. For once perhaps we manage to penetrate the world inhabited by Crivelli characters—a world which does not become more cordial, but definitely more human. The grim face of the hermit Honofrius reveals to us that Crivelli's art was not always splendid and unattainable, outside the realms of time. (*N.G.*)

Beatrice Cenci. The Sad Fate of Oppressed Innocence

The tragic story of this young Roman noblewoman (1577–1599), as told in Muratori's chronicles and Guerrazzi's historical novel, would stir the compassion of such Romantic writers as Shelley, Stendhal and Dumas, whose own works recount the story of this heroine, the only one in a family of cowards that dared to stand up to a cruel father and paid the ultimate price for her courage. Francesco Cenci was one of the richest men in Rome, but he was also violent and dissolute. Fearing that the marriage of his long-suffering daughter Beatrice would undermine his wealth— already sorely tried by the losses resulting from his sons' speculative investments and the fines resulting from his own riotous behaviour—he locked Beatrice away with her stepmother in the castle of Petrella Salto near Rieti. Driven to desperation by the continual beatings that even this desolate location did not spare her, the girl—together with her gaoler, who may also have become her lover—organized her father's murder, planning it to look an accident. However, there were quickly a number of rumours concerning the real cause of the man's death and an inquiry led to the arrest of Beatrice and her brothers (whom she had imprudently informed of her plan). Tortured, she confessed; and her trial was followed by a Rome both horrified and moved by her story. However, in spite of this public sympathy, her fate was sealed by Clement VIII's determination to seize the family's confiscated property, and the girl was executed at Ponte Sant'Angelo in September 1599 before a huge crowd that was deeply moved by the youth of the victim and her courage before the executioner. One of those spectators may have been Caravaggio, who took the beheading of the young woman as the inspiration for his own *Judith Beheading Holofernes*, where the realism of even the smallest anatomical detail in the severed neck suggests the work must have been based on close observation. (*N.G.*)

Beatrice Cenci in a portrait that is attributed to Guido Reni and was part of the Barberini Collection. Galleria Nazionale d'Arte Antica, Rome. The unlucky girl, whose splendid brown hair is enveloped in a white turban, is shown glancing towards the viewer like an innocent, bemused victim.

Coming back to the Apollo Room, the door opposite leads, via a narrow passageway cut through the walls, to the **Justice Chamber**. The massive even-sized blocks that make up the walls here are a reminder that we are back in the heart of the original mausoleum, directly above the Urn Chamber. Immediately in front as you enter is a fresco that may depict St. Michael the Archangel or may be an allegory of Justice (it has recently been attributed to Zaga). As one can see from the fact that the painting is truncated, this chamber must originally have been taller and had probably been used as a chapel; it was then used for trials and the announcement of verdicts and sentences. Imagining the whole thing as it might appear in some swashbuckling film set, one can visualize the judges' bench at the far end of the room, with the severe magistrate pronouncing a sentence of death whilst above him towers a figure who might be an imposing allegory of Justice or represent the agent of divine wrath (it really makes no difference). And the prisoners brought here to hear their fate might be common criminals; cardinals guilty of plotting against the pope; or hapless humanists, such as Platina or Pomponio Leto. Then, of course, there were the exceptionally famous cases: it was in this grim chamber that Clement VIII ordered that Giordano Bruno be burnt alive, and it was here that—in spite of her tender age and the number of attenuating circumstances accompanying her crime—he handed down a death sentence on the patricide Beatrice Cenci. Nowadays the room temporarily houses a small collection of artillery dating from this period.
Passing back through the Apollo Room and out through a narrow doorway on the left, we come to a wide, half-moon-shaped

The Justice Chamber.

courtyard that occupies the top of the first cylinder of the mausoleum. However, before exploring here, turn right through a tiny doorway that leads by a steep staircase to the Bathhouse of Clement VII, one of the hidden jewels of the Castle. (*N.G.*)

The Bathhouse of Clement VII
This unusual combination of rooms is linked to the papal apartments by an internal staircase. The main space is made up of what is known as the Bathhouse of Clement VII, named after the pope who commissioned the decoration. It is linked to a changing-room, on the floor above, and a boiler-room, where stoves heated the water which ran through pipes under the floor of the bathhouse and thus maintained it at a pleasant temperature. As Bruno Contardi mentions in his study of the Bathhouse of Clement VII, during the first half of the sixteenth century it was a common thing for such a facility (known as a *stufa* or *stuffetta*) to be installed in princely residences—as examples, one might cite those in the Ducal

Palace of Urbino or that created within the Vatican for Cardinal Bernardo Bibbiena (around 1515, this was decorated with frescoes to original designs by Raphael). Obviously, such facilities were the privilege of the wealthy. However, the creation of a bathhouse equipped with running water was more than just a demonstration of affluence. The architecture and decoration of the space underlined the status of the Renaissance prince as a man imbued with classical culture (after all, the Romans had had a passion for *thermae*) and equally dedicated to the refined pleasures of mind and body. It is no coincidence that the scholars who have studied such facilities have drawn a parallel between bathhouses and *studioli*, those small studios to which princes retired in order to enjoy their libraries and art collections in solitude. Given this, perhaps one of the most significant things about the Bathhouse of Clement VII is its location—a clear illustration that the sixteenth-century pontiffs wanted their apartments within the Castle to enjoy all the comforts and elegance of a princely residence even though they were sited in what was a military stronghold. It seems certain that the first plans for a bathroom in Castel Sant'Angelo date back to the beginning on the sixteenth century, even if the space that has come down to us is that created for the Aldobrandini pope who gives his name to it. The structure itself can be dated between 1525 and 1536: the coats-of-arms on the vault also include that of the Castle Governor, Guido de' Medici, who was appointed in 1525 and, upon his swearing-in, had an inventory drawn up of the Castle's rooms and contents which contains no mention of a bathroom (the facility is, however, mentioned in a 1536 description of Castel Sant'Angelo written by Johannes Fichard, who seems to

suggest it was already in operation). These dates would seem to rule out the frequently-credited attribution of the decoration to Giulio Romano: he had left Rome a long time before they can have been painted. Much more probable is the attribution given by Vasari: to Giovanni da Udine, who may however have worked to designs prepared by Giulio Romano before his flight from Rome upon the arrival of the German mercenaries in 1527. The Castel Sant'Angelo Bathhouse is in a rectangular space (c. 2.60 × 1.5 m) aligned lengthways north-south. Now closed by a grille, the entrance is in the west wall and surmounted by the inscription CLEMENS VII P.M.; the one source of natural light is the marble-framed window in the north wall. In effect, the bathhouse is made of two communicating rooms: the first, immediately after the entrance, has a panelled vault and smooth walls decorated with three coats-of-arms in stucco; the second, smaller, room, has a coffered barrel vault and contains the bathtub proper, which rests on a marble base and is trimmed with the same type of marble. In the first room, the longer walls contain large frescoed niches decorated with stucco shells. There are also three smaller niches around the bathtub: the two side ones are at the same height as the larger, whilst that in the east wall is placed higher, above the existing tubes for hot and cold water (the former is on the right, given that the tubes ran through the, more sheltered, internal wall on the south side of the room). The fresco and stucco decoration is entirely based on aquatic motifs, articulated to follow the complex structure of this small architectural gem, underlining both its separation into different spaces and its overall cohesion. To make it easier to follow, this description of the frescoes starts with the lower part of the wall and then moves upwards.

The lower frieze is made up of a band of rectangular panels with putti, dolphins, swans and plant motifs, framed by a fake socle that continues the motif of the base and moulding of the bath tub. The space between the niches above the socle is frescoed with a series of seven panels that depict the thrones of the major deities of Olympus, who the artist shows as accompanying the pontiff in his ablutions. The deities are not portrayed directly but are recognisable because the robes and attributes they have abandoned on their way to bathe are shown draped over their thrones. Proceeding from the entrance, the first throne on the north wall (to the left) is shown with the winged helmet and caduceus (rod of intertwined serpents) that identify Mercury, messenger of the gods and protector of trade; in the festoons above is a magpie, probably a reference to the fact that Mercury was also the protector of thieves. On the next throne are the helmet, sceptre and eagle that are associated with Jupiter, whose presence/absence is also depicted in the second panel on the right wall. The last throne bears the quiver, bow and musical instruments that serve to identify Apollo.

Moving in the same direction along the opposite wall, one comes first to a throne with a female robe, sandals and a laurel crown, with a fish shown in the festoons above: this has often been taken as indicating Venus, but it seems more likely that the reference is to Nike, goddess of victory,

The Bathhouse of Clement VII.

The Leo X Courtyard.

View of the central tower of the Castle from the Well Courtyard. On the right are the traces of the work undertaken in 1970 by D'Onofrio to ascertain if the original fastigium of Hadrian's structure was circular.

even if one cannot be certain and the significance of the fish remains a mystery. Then, as already mentioned, comes another reference to Jupiter, followed by an indecipherable image. On the entrance wall itself—unfortunately not visible to modern-day visitors behind the grille—are the helmet, lance, breastplate and shield that serve to identify Mars, god of War; above the throne is a cockerel. Each panel is framed by a festoon of plant motifs which extends the length of all of the walls, thus

consolidating the unity of the entire decorative scheme. Above the bowl-shaped vaults of the niches are four panels depicting mythological stories that serve to heighten the joyful and vaguely erotic atmosphere of the entire place. On the left wall, closest to the doorway, is the scene of *Vulcan watching Venus as she awaits Mars*, the betrayed husband shown holding the fine net which, Homer and Ovid tell us, he will cast over the lovers to then expose them to the ridicule of the other gods. The meaning of the second scene is not clear, but it shows a woman (Venus?) and a winged youth (Cupid?) alongside a fountain in a garden. Along the southern wall, again proceeding from the doorway, there is a rare combination of Diana, the virgin goddess of hunting (here shown with her hounds), and Cupid, who is depicted stealing an arrow from her quiver, perhaps to move in conquest against the tower/castle shown in the background (such structures were common allegories of virginity). The scene, therefore, would seem to suggest an attack upon Virtue by the god of Eros. The last panel shows four figures, perhaps putti and nymphs, who are looking into an expanse of water; here again the actual meaning the scene is unclear. The other panels on the walls and vault are decorated with friezes and grotesques, the predominance of white at the lower levels serving to heighten the luminous effects of the gilding above. (*L.B.*)

The bathhouse itself separates the semi-circular courtyard from the delightful **Leo X Courtyard** that opens to the left. Created around 1514 for this Medici pope, the space is also known as the Boiler Courtyard because it houses the boilers used to heat the water for the bathhouse above (one can see the opening for the tubes in the wall). Once adorned with a beautifully-kept Italian Garden, this courtyard is overlooked by the beautiful transom and mullion windows of the apartment we have already visited, whilst further up the wall there is an open loggia. The courtyard is associated not only with Leo X, but also Julius II (there are three fine coats-of-arms of his Della Rovere family)—two highly-learned and cultured pontiffs who played a leading role in the great period of the Renaissance in Rome.

Now we return to what is known as the **Theatre Courtyard**; it was probably used for plays in the time of Leo X. A frieze of festoons and putti runs between the rectangular windows that crown the exedra built opposite the central tower; these windows were also linked with the lower openings alongside the doors of that structure by (now badly damaged) graffito work based on the twenty engravings of the *Deities of Fable* which Caraglio produced in 1526 on the basis of original drawings by Rosso Fiorentino. Various sixteenth-century sources confirm the presence in this space of tall trees: besides the above-mentioned notebook of the German traveller Fichard, there is also a fresco by Montano which depicts the scene of the appearance of the Angel on the Castle—complete with trees— and at various points in his *Life*, a work to which we will return, Benvenuto Cellini makes references to such vegetation. The embankment discovered beneath this level (similar to the more substantial earthworks found under the Angel Courtyard) is taken by those who argue the mausoleum was modelled on an Etruscan burial tumulus as being the surviving remnants of what was, in Roman days, a hanging garden of evergreens. It is true that this area was well-supplied with water—as one can see from the fine well-head decorated around 1501 with the crest of the Borgia pope Alexander VI (the inside of the well has equally fine decoration).

The Theatre Courtyard with the graffito-decorated buildings.

Marble well-head decorated
with Borgia devices, now
in the "Well Courtyard."

The steps down
from the Well Courtyard
to the Prisons.

Marble well-head decorated with Borgia devices, now in the "Well Courtyard."

In order to embellish his fortress, this pope commissioned a wholesale scheme of work involving the entire Castle—think, for example, of the spectacular ramp that runs in an oblique line over the burial chamber itself—and for the 1500 Jubilee had the Ponte Sant'Angelo repaved, as well as opening the Via Alessandrina that was intended to link the fortress with the Vatican palaces. He was also the pontiff who commissioned Pinturicchio to paint frescoes of his own life-story in various rooms of the Castle; however, of these *Istorie di Papa Alessandro*, which Vasari tells us were rich in portraits and grotesque-motif decoration, all that remains is a preparatory drawing now in the Louvre (thanks to which we can date the work at around 1494–98). Although much of the Borgia pope's work on the Castle would be destroyed by the subsequent alterations commissioned by Urban VIII in the first half of the seventeenth century, Alexander VI's mark can still be seen in this area of the Castle: directly under this courtyard are five storage spaces for grain hollowed out within the circular wall of the drum (these are still referred to by the Spanish name

of *silos*), as well as two large spaces intended to house an enormous cistern whose three interconnecting chambers were used to purify oil through filtering and the waters of the Tiber through sedimentation. The large travertine manhole covers with their metal rings which one can see dotted around the paving here gave access to these tanks and granaries, where essential supplies might be stored in case of siege (for security reasons, these lower spaces are—like the famous prisons—not open to the general visitor. However, every Sunday there are guided tours for small groups). The stone balls one now sees piled up in the courtyard were not actually fired from cannon

The steps down from the Well Courtyard to the Prisons.

but dropped from the battlements, to smash wooded siege-towers wheeled up to the walls below.

The Castle Dungeons

You can almost hear the clink of the prisoners' chains as you walk down into the large rectangular space of the parlatory. From there you pass into a corridor whose semi-circular wall contains three low doorways into grim cells, where the only sources of light are narrow, barred windows that open out at ground level in the Well Courtyard. Known as the **"historic gaols,"** these were the places where many spent their final night before execution (the last prisoners to do so were Risorgimento patriots, condemned for their opposition to the temporal power of the papacy). Passing on, one comes to another two cells, in which traces of the crown of the Roman wall have recently been discovered. One of the occupants of the second cell was Benvenuto Cellini, who spent more than one year here and in his *Life* (I, 120) tells how he drew a God the Father and a Resurrected Christ on the wall to provide himself with a source of consolation.

The room was also that closest to the water-tank, which must have leaked as the artist complains not only of the darkness but of the "great quantity of water." Continuing along the corridor

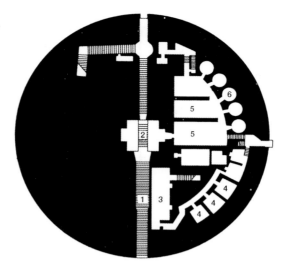

one comes to a small room where, on the right, is an external latrine which is said to be that Cellini used for his famous escape. On the left, one descends below the level of the courtyard to the two huge oil storerooms, where eighty-three terracotta urns contained the oil that was used for cooking and as lighting fuel, but might well become a terrible weapon when heated and poured over the enemies who were trying to scale the walls (it was only in the twentieth century that these vats were fitted into the cement). Passing through a large empty room, one then comes to five circular pits; these were used to store grain, which will have been poured down into these containers just as the oil was poured down into the vats. (*N.G.*)

Plan of the second floor of the Castle.

1. Diametric ramp
2. Urn Chamber
3. Parlatory
4. Historic Gaols
5. Oil Storerooms
6. Silos

The curved access corridor linking the cells of the prison.

Inside one of the cells.

Passionate and heroic, but also irascible and violent, the great Florentine sculptor and goldsmith had eventually to flee his native city, but thanks to his gifts received a ready welcome in Rome at the court of the Medici popes—and that of Leo X in particular. Having entered the papal service as a musician, he would pass memorable days locked in the Castle together with Clement VII during the terrible 1527 Sack of Rome, when—given his great skill with weapons—he served both as an harquebusier and artillery-man in the defence of the fortress, and even claims to have played a part in the death of the officer commanding the besieging troops, Charles Bourbon, and in the wounding of his successor, the Prince of Orange (*Life*, I, 34–37). However, the narrative contained in his autobiography is rather fanciful, and though never actually disproved cannot be conclusively confirmed either. In this first extract from that exuberant life story, he boasts of his skill as a marksman, which earned him the praise of the pontiff himself.

"I pursued my business of artilleryman, and every day performed some extraordinary feat, whereby the credit and the favor I acquired with the pope was something indescribable. There never passed a day but what I killed one or another of our enemies in the besieging army. On one occasion the pope was walking round the circular keep, when he observed a Spanish colonel in the Prati; he recognized the man by certain indications, seeing that this officer had formerly been in his service; and while he fixed his eyes on him, he kept talking about him. I, above by the Angel, spied a fellow down there, busying himself about the trenches with a javelin in his hand; he was dressed entirely in rose-colour; and so studying the worse I could, I selected a gerfalcon; it is larger and longer than a swivel, and about the size of a demi-culverin. This I emptied, and loaded it with a good charge of fine powder mixed with the coarser sort; then I aimed it exactly at the man in red, elevating prodigiously, because a piece of that calibre could hardly be expected to carry true at such a distance. I fired, and hit my man exactly in the middle. He had trussed his sword in front, for swagger, after a way those Spaniards have; and my ball broke upon the blade, and one could see the fellow cut in two fair halves. The pope, who expecting nothing of this kind, derived great pleasure and amazement from the sight, both because it seemed to him impossible that one should aim and hit the mark at such a distance, and also because the man was cut in two, and he could not comprehend how this should happen. He sent for me, and asked about it. I explained all the device I had used in firing; but told him that why the man was cut in halves, neither he nor I could know. Upon my bended knees I then besought him to give me the pardon for that homicide; and for all the others I had committed in the Castle in service of the Church. Thereat the pope, raising his hand, and making a large open sign of the cross upon my face, told me that he gave me pardon for all murders I had ever perpetrated, or should ever perpetrate in the service of the Apostolic Church" (*Life* I, 37). Castel Sant'Angelo re-appears in his life in 1538, when the murder of his brother's murderer and—more importantly—Pier Luigi Farnese's accusation that Cellini had stolen some of the jewels of Clement VII, led to the artist coming back to the fortress as a prisoner. He would not be there long. In the custody of a mad

Castle Governor who thought he was a bat, Cellini dreamt up an escape plan that stretches belief to the limit. He first began by not returning his dirty bed linen, hiding the sheets under his mattress (claiming that he was keeping them as a gift for the poor soldiery). Having cut them into strips, he sewed them together into a long rope and, with a pair of tongs he had in the meantime stole from his gaoler, he one night pulled out the nails that held his door and then fixed them back in place with wax, so that no one could tell the door was practically off its hinges. At this point, everything was ready for his escape. The night of a festivity in the Castle he was probably accompanied as far as the exit of the drum by an accomplice. At the drawbridge, he tied the sheets to one of the merlons and dropped down to the ground, making off to the house of Cardinal Cornaro even though he had a broken leg. Recaptured and brought back to the Castle, he was thrown into a dark, humid cell he complains of in these terms:

I was taken underneath a garden to a very dark room, which was full of water, spiders and poisonous snakes. I was thrown onto a filthy mattress on the ground, given nothing to eat that evening, and closed behind four doors. And thus I was until seven o'clock the next day. Then I was brought food, and I asked that they give me some of my books to read. None of them talked to me, but they did pass on the request to the poor Castle Governor, who had asked what I had said. The next morning I was given my Bible in Italian and another book that included Giovan Villani's Chronicles. Asking for some of my other books, I was told that I would not get any more and that what I had was already too much. So I lived unhappily on that soaking mattress, and within three days everything was wet. I still could not move, because I had a broken leg, and wanting to get out of the bed because of the needs of my excrement, I went on all fours with great difficulty so that I would not soil the place where I slept. I had an hour and a half of light each day, a pale reflection of light that came into that unhappy cellar through a very small window; and only then could I read. The rest of the day and night I was patiently in the darkness, but God was never out of my thoughts, nor the fraility of human life. I was sure that in a few days my unlucky existence would come to an end in there" (*Life*, I, 117).

But it didn't. Luck was on his side once more: a short time later, the king of France, a great admirer of his work, convinced the pope to set him free. Thus, Benvenuto could return to the tumultuous life which would finally end in death by misadventure.

His great autobiography brings together anachronistic references to objects, institutions and practices; it is filled with characters that really have nothing to do with the story, inexplicable episodes, rare words that are mistaken for misprints and misunderstood references... And yet, in spite of the boasting and the wilfully ungrammatical Italian, Cellini manages to project the same impression of himself as that one receives from his works, appearing as "the best," the creator of masterpieces. Ironically, perhaps the only extant portrait of a man who dedicated so much to his self-image is the work of someone else: a painting by Vasari, now in the Palazzo Vecchio in Florence. (*N.G.*)

Stairs at the end of the Theatre
Courtyard take one up to the
Library Vestibule, where the
ceiling is still decorated with
fragments of frescoes. From
here one enters the magnificent
Library. Sixteenth-century
account-books refer to this
room solely as the "the new
room looking towards Prati"
or the "painted room," and the
modern name most probably
derives from the fact that it was
used to store papal documents
(which in 1799 were all
transferred to the Vatican).
A spacious room with a vaulted
ceiling, this stands in the
northern part of the Farnese
apartments; its northern end
is linked to the rooms
of the mausoleum proper,
whilst the southern end leads
into the Treasury. As with the rest
of this wing of the Castle, the
decorations were painted between
1543 and 1545. Here, they are the
work of Luzio Luzi of Todi, who
had worked with Perin del Vaga
on the frescoes of the Genoese
Palazzo Doria in 1528–33.
Luzi's responsibility both
for designing the frescoes and
overseeing their execution is
proved by the existence of notes
of payment and numerous
preparatory sketches (the latter
now in the British Museum

and the Windsor Royal Library).
This fascinating decorative
scheme is still striking, both
for its rich variety of images
and its combination of frescoes
and stucco alto-relievo. The
best-preserved part of the entire
decoration is the vault; rising
from a frieze with scenes of
sacrificial offerings and deities,
this comprises a symmetrical
arrangement of square,
octagonal, oval and round panels
set against a painted background
of grotesque motifs. The frames
of the panels—along with the
splendid frieze that runs around
the top of the four walls—are all
stucco-work, and the panels
themselves are decorated with
lively renderings of episodes
from the history of Rome and
the life of Hadrian, together
with allegorical and mythological
scenes. As in all the other rooms
of the papal apartments, those
who commissioned the work
and those who produced it were
aiming not only to delight the eye
but also to communicate a
message, the meaning of which
would have been clearly
understandable to an educated
sixteenth-century visitor, but
understandable today only thanks
to historical analysis: scholars
have established that the
politicians, ambassadors and
foreign heads of state who were
received by the pope in the Castel
Sant'Angelo apartments were,
in effect, being presented with
a clear propaganda statement
of Paul III's political and cultural
claims and aspirations. The
artistic language used here was
that Mannerist style whose peak
of popularity can be said to have
come in the 1540s. Appreciated
for the density of its learned
cultural references and its use of
grandiose—if sometimes
strained—pictorial compositions,
that style was used here in works
whose every single detail was

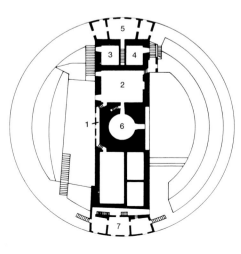

carefully studied to convey the self-image that Alessandro Farnese wished to project.

The dominant theme in all the Castel Sant'Angelo frescoes is the celebration of the pontiff as the heir of the ancient emperors—Hadrian, above all—and the restorer of Rome's greatness. It should be remembered that after the trauma of the Sack of Rome (1527) and the Lutheran schism, the Church was once more asserting the legitimacy of a universal order under the aegis of Catholicism—and the man who commissioned these frescoes was putting himself forward as the person to lead such a restoration. Paul III aimed to present himself as a new Hadrian, a magnificent prince committed to reviving the fortunes of the Church of Rome and making the city itself once more the capital of an empire. Hence, in the decoration of the Castle he insisted on a continuity between his own reign and that of the ancient emperor who had consolidated the frontiers of dominions under external threat; had assimilated the cultures of the peoples he subjugated; and had instilled new vigour into the ancient traditions of Classical Rome. Seen from this point of view,

the Library is one of the main chapters in a complex text of images intended to celebrate the legendary origins of the capital of the empire; and these references to Classical Antiquity were to be seen in both the subject-matter of the decoration and the artistic styles and techniques chosen to produce it. The imagery of the vault is dominated by the events linked with the foundation of Rome, the city's gradual emancipation from Etruscan hegemony and its own assertion of military might over the entire peninsula. And these events ran in parallel to the emergence of the political and ethnic unity of the Romans as a people—a fact which Hadrian himself had significantly chosen to reiterate by encouraging the use of patriotic images in coins, medallions and large-scale works of sculpture.

The sources used by those who designed the decoration for the Castle were undoubtedly the poets and annalists of the Augustan Age, whose presentation of events was shrouded in an atmosphere of legend and fable—an atmosphere

Luzio Luzi and assistants, *Crest of Paul III Set between Allegorical Figures of the Church and Rome*, preparatory drawing. British Museum, London (n. 1964).

Luzio Luzi and assistants, *Frieze with Scenes of Religious Sacrifices*, stucco (detail). Library.

Luzio Luzi and assistants, *The Emperor Hadrian*, fresco. Library.

Luzio Luzi and assistants,
*Horatius Cocles at the Sublicius
Bridge*, fresco. Library.

Luzio Luzi and assistants,
Episodes from the Life of Hadrian,
panel with idealised
depiction of the Mausoleum
and the Pons Aelius, fresco.
Library.

that was heightened here by the use of a rather fantastic artistic language.

In the centre of the vault stands the marble coat-of-arms of Paul III, to the sides of which are the Farnese symbols of the fleur-de-lis (emblem of Justice) and a young girl with a unicorn. This is the very crux of the entire decoration scheme, and is clearly placed in relation to the two images of Hadrian and Michael the Archangel located between grotesque motifs on either side of the vault, a visual juxtaposition that "shows" the political actions of the pope as sealing together the worlds of Classical tradition and Christian faith.

This historical continuity between the city and the papacy is further underlined by the repetition of Paul III's coat-of-arms above the large fireplace, where it is flanked by allegories of the Church and Rome. The latter is shown on the right holding Victory in her hand, but having laid down her weapons. The message is clear: greatness is

achieved by military might, but preserved through the extraordinary force of a universal civilisation. Moving outwards from the centre of the vault, there are oval stucco panels decorated with various Roman gods: *Mars and Neptune* to the east, *Pan with a Nymph and Hercules* to the south; a *Calf-Bearer and Minerva* to the west; and *Peace and the Goddess Roma* to the north. Between the side panels of *Episodes from the Life of Hadrian* are semi-lunettes frescoed with mythological scenes: to the north, *Pan Chased Away by a Nymph* and *Venus between Cupid and Pan*; to the south *Pan Playing his Pipe for a Nymph and a Youth* and the *Metamorphosis of Daphne*. On the end walls, above the images of St. Michael the Archangel and Hadrian there is more of the same subject: *Pan and a She-Goat*. The narration of the legends regarding the founding of Rome starts from the two panels on the long side of the vault alongside the central rectangle. On the north side is *The Capture of Veio*, an Etruscan city taken by Furius Camillus by means of a ploy; and on the south, the *Punishment of Tarpea*, the girl who was guardian of the Capitoline castle but opened the city gates to the invading Sabines. Above a marine-motif frieze, the short ends of the room are decorated with stories linked to the expulsion from Rome of the Tarquins, the last kings of Etruscan descent. In spite of the poor state of preservation, one can recognise: *The Flight of Clelia*; *Rhea Sylvia and the Twins Romulus and Remus* (?); *Horatius Cocles on the Pons Sublicius*; and *Mucius Scaevola in the Camp of Porsenna*. In the background of this latter one can recognise the south front of the Castel Sant'Angelo.

The propaganda message is then reinforced by four episodes from the *Life of Hadrian* depicted alongside the frieze, which some scholars have identified as showing the emperor's search for a suitable site for his mausoleum. Here, the taste for classical, archaeological motifs could be given full expression in the depiction of various classical buildings which—like the Paul III Loggia—are shown in an idealised, fantastic form; in effect, they are compendia of details of decoration and construction taken from various buildings of the second century AD. The one exception is the depiction of the *Pons Aelius* in the panel on the south wall; this draws on an old image that has come down to us (that on a medallion from the time of Hadrian which is now in the Museo Correr in Venice). The ideologically-inspired decoration of the papal apartments continues in the frescoes of the Sala Paolina, where it achieves a coherence that was perhaps beyond the capacities of the group of artists headed by Luzi. However, what makes the decoration of the Library so fascinating is its wealth of decorative techniques and the very density of the references to Classical Antiquity. The scenes depicted are drawn from mythology and Classical history, whilst the decorative framework within which they appear is itself modelled on the art of the Imperial Age, with the use of painted grotesque motifs and an alternation of frescoes and stucco alto-relievo (a combination that the artists of the sixteenth century would have known from the rooms of the Domus Aurea). (*L.B.*) A doorway at the end of north wall of the Library leads through into the **Hadrianeum Room**.

The name is an invention of Borgatti's—the original use of the space is unknown—and is due to the fact that during restoration work he carried out here, a depiction of Hadrian's Mausoleum came to light (on the upper part of the wall opposite the entrance). The image shows a building of four cubic solids on top of the other, adorned with niches for statues and surmounted by a quadriga driven by a male figure; this stands amidst fronds which are said to represent the funeral garden that

Luzio Luzi and assistants, *Cornice of Animals and Marine Deities*, vault fresco. Library.

Prospero Fontana (attr.) *Idealised Depiction of Hadrian's Mausoleum*, from the frieze in the Hadrianeum Room.

Sixteenth-century artist (copy of original by Giorgione and Titian), *Bacchanal*, oil on canvas. Museo Nazionale di Castel Sant'Angelo.

was on the top of the mausoleum. The structure thus depicted has the form of a *pyrae* as it appears on the back of Roman *consecratio* coins (representations which in the sixteenth century were taken to be depictions of mausolea). During the Renaissance, such coins—and antiquarian objects generally—became one source of inspiration for painted decoration. Hence, between 1544 and 1545, Luzio Luzi designed (though perhaps Prospero Fontana painted) the frescoed frieze showing "archaeological" reconstructions of other Roman monuments within golden frames; these are delimited by pairs of white caryatids and modest telamones which are rather strangely attired. A study of the literary, documentary and archaeological material available to these artists enables us to identify some of these structures with parts of the *Ager Vaticanus* that have already been mentioned: the *Meta Romuli*, the *Naumachia* and the *Circus of Caligula and Nero* (complete with obelisk). These period "postcards" fit in perfectly with the satyrs, fauns, sileni and cupids that mark out the rhythm of the unfolding frieze. (*N.G.*)

In this room there are three paintings of Bacchus, attributed to Dosso Dossi, Nicolas Poussin and the Dutch artist Jacob Jordaens. The Dossi picture shows a group of figures in the foreground within an extraordinary landscape setting; the luminosity of the colour and the intensity of the light-effects reveal the artist's great interest in the work of contemporary Venetian painters. Dosso Dossi lived in Ferrara from around 1470 to c. 1542, and participated in the prestigious project for the decoration of Alfonso d'Este's *camerino*, having been called—along with Titian—to replace Giovanni Bellini and Raphael. This *camerino* was a Renaissance *studiolo*, a private space to which the prince retired in order to read or enjoy his art collection in private. In Ferrara, Duke Alfonso I intended to have his *studiolo* decorated with a number of paintings of scenes involving the god Bacchus, which were commissioned from the greatest artists of the day—Fra' Bartolomeo, Giovanni Bellini and Raphael; however, the latter two died before they delivered their work, and so Titian and Dosso Dossi were appointed to replace them. The theme was perfectly suited to the fashions of the day and to the taste for classical quotations which were intended to underline the culture and erudition of the prince—as well as suggesting parallels between him and the deities of Olympus. Initially attributed to Giorgione, the Castel Sant'Angelo *Bacchanal* was long identified with the work that Dossi produced for the Duke of Ferrara (but it now seems that the Ferrara picture is that which hangs in the London National Gallery). The second picture in this room—another *Bacchanal*—is of dubious attribution: rather than being an original Poussin, it is probably a just good copy of the of the above-mentioned painting that Giovanni Bellini and Titian produced for the d'Este *camerino*. The third painting—the *Education of Bacchus*—shows the god as a child in the company of the tigress that suckled him, the satyr Silenus and another play fellow. The picture comes from Genoa, a city that attracted such high calibre Flemish artists as Rubens and Van Dyck, and where the flourishing local school of painting quickly assimilated what was to be learnt from the art of Northern Europe. Recently the attribution to Jacob Jordaens has been questioned, with the resurrection of a previous theory that the work was by an artist of the Rubens circle. The room also contains a copy of Lorenzo Lotto's *Madonna and Child between St. Roch and St. John,* and a small fifteenth-century painting of a cupid. This latter has been identified as a *desco da parto,* which were very common in fifteenth-century Tuscany. Generally round in form, these *deschi* were used as trays on which to present food and gifts to a woman just after childbirth, and hence were usually decorated with images linked to the theme of birth and childhood. (*L.B.*)

Lorenzo Lotto, *St. Jerome in the Wilderness*, c. 1509, oil on panel, 80.5 × 61 cm, signed on the rock to the lower right: L. LOTVS. Donated to the Castel Sant'Angelo Museum in 1916 by Count Menotti.

"... this I can tell you that my mind is in such a turmoil that it will be very difficult for me to calm my soul..."
Lorenzo Lotto

Of great importance because it is the only picture we know certainly to have been painted by Lotto during the artist's rather mysterious but decisive stay in Rome, this work and its history are exhaustively described in the catalogue to the 1983 Lotto exhibition held at Castel Sant'Angelo. That volume also gives invaluable information regarding the state of the picture after the 1970 restoration (there is considerable warping of the panel, which has resulted in numerous cracks down the length of the painting). The work is certainly later than the small devotional image with *St. Jerome the Penitent*, now in the Louvre, which the artist may have painted upon commission for the bishop of Treviso de' Rossi (in 1506?). The popularity of this theme amongst Renaissance artists was, in fact, one of the reasons why it eventually became popular with patrons themselves. However, in this return to the theme, one can clearly see a radical change due to the influence not only of Giovanni Bellini and Antonello da Messina, but also of Giorgione. Whilst the Louvre *St. Jerome* combines the two classical iconographies of the saint—as a penitent and a contemplative figure—here he actually "duplicates" his representation to show both aspects of the saint in distinct figures: Jerome is shown amongst the rocks as a penitent, gazing upon the Crucifix whilst he grasps the stone with which he will beat his breast, and—in the foreground of the painting—as a hoary-haired saint, a round-headed old man with a flowing beard shown amidst books at the foot of a tree that stands at the side of some crudely-fenced road. The saint now is a firmly-modelled presence in the painting, and is no longer squashed into the rocky background. This—and the more classical rendition of the figure—clearly reveal the influence of the artist's stay in Rome, which was one rich in experimentation and new encounters. Lotto had perhaps been invited to the city by Bramante, who had worked in Loreto as an architect around the end of 1508 and must have been favourably struck by the polyptych that the artist—not yet thirty years old—had painted for the church of San Domenico in nearby Recanati. Various notes of payment reveal that in 1509 the painter collaborated on the decoration of Julius II's new papal apartments in the Vatican, working alongside such artists as Perugino, Sodoma, Bramantino and, of course, Raphael. Although sources say that once the clear supremacy of Raphael was recognised, the works of the other artists were removed, there have been numerous attempts to identify parts of the Stanze frescoes as the actual work of Lotto himself; however, that argument is far too tricky to be explored here. David Alan Brown has, however, been able to identify the debts which Lotto in this *St. Jerome* owed to the other artists, who had became a source of inspiration in his own work. The borrowing from the trapezoidal panels decorating the vault of the Segnatura is very clear: look at the composition of the reclining figure to the left—almost a sort of river god—who is shown in a rocky landscape with a tree (the satyr that spies from behind drapery in the Sodoma painting is, in Lotto's work, transformed into that mild-natured lion that was said to have been devoted to the saint after he had removed a thorn from his paw). And again, when drawing inspiration from the partially-draped figure of the reclining Diogenes in Raphael's *School of Athens*, Lotto manages to make the result very much his own. Just as the Greek philosopher is holding a manuscript in his left hand, so the figure of St. Jerome is shown elegantly leafing through the book on the ground before him; however, the profile of the hermit is actually taken—identical—from the representation of the selfsame saint seated to the side

of the altar in the *Discussion of the Sacrament*. These deliberate quotations of Raphael support the dating of this panel at around 1509–10—before, that is, the painter began to feel that he was in the right place at the wrong time (something that would happen throughout his life): aware he was emerging the loser from comparisons he felt were unfair, Lotto would in fact flee Rome in a state of total doubt as to his own worth. As Brown pointed out: "this synthesis of both pagan and religious sources in Lotto's work was perfectly suited to the very figure of St. Jerome, the prototype of the Christian humanist," the translator of the Bible, a refined exegete who was thoroughly conversant with the works of Classical Antiquity. The quiet that emanates from the scholar amongst his books can also be felt in the landscape. The rocks to the left, where the insistent line reveals the clear influence of Dürer's engravings, is still reminiscent of the Paris *St. Jerome*. However, the tenebrous opening in the background, which is faintly lit by the pink light of a distant sunset, seems to herald a more northern feel for the natural world. The tree, an almost evanescent presence seen against the cloud-streaked sky above the valley, reveals a full grasp of that deep sensitivity to atmosphere which was such a part of the work of Raphael and the art of Central Italy. The ascetic life of the saint, with its tensions and its continual search for salvation, is here set within a context of natural forces that highlight the solitude of the efforts being made by the single individual. There is a sort of ambiguous anthropomorphism, for example, in the depiction of some of the natural features: the truncated tree in the foreground combines surreal female forms that seem to evoke the temptations of the flesh against which Jerome had struggled; and the roots of the trees on the overhang behind the saint have something diabolical about them in their similarity to deformed human hands. Every

single painting produced by this mysterious artist seems to become an enigma that has to be resolved. Careful observation always turns up some symbol to be deciphered, one of those alchemical "signatures" that make Lotto's artistic language sometimes seem that it is addressed solely to the initiated. How, therefore, is one to read the wood-cutter, the shepherd with his flocks and—especially—the mule being beaten by its owner? The distant view of the walled city by a river is probably an allusion to the urban life that has been fled in pursuit of spiritual renewal. That city is Rome; and amongst the buildings is a round fortified structure that is clearly a poetic rendition of Castel Sant'Angelo on the banks of the Tiber, which Lotto would have seen many times from the windows of the Vatican. For Jerome, Rome had been the place of youthful studies, where the apprenticeship in grammar and rhetoric went hand-in-hand with a pleasure-loving existence in which there was little room for contemplation or asceticism. He would return there in 382, appointed secretary to Pope Damasus, but as a very different person. No longer tolerating compromise and meanness of spirit, he was now someone dedicated to the ideal of an austere life: in fact, upon the death of his patron he would be obliged to leave the city in indignation after the Roman clergy—the object of his frequent criticisms—rose up against him in physical rebellion. The artist may therefore have seen the desolate solitude of Jerome—a theme that was so dear to him: he dealt with it in at least five works—as a metaphor for his own spiritual condition. For a sensitive, restless wanderer fascinated by the complexities of human psychology, the figure of the saint will have embodied all his secret aspirations. Like Jerome, he too was attracted by the monastic life, and his art—imbued as it is with a clear, evangelical Christianity—was his own way on making the Scriptures available to the populace. (*N.G.*)

Raphael, Diogenes reclining of the steps in *The School of Athens* (detail). Stanza della Segnatura, Vatican City.

The fine brickwork visible behind the cabinets dates from the period of Hadrian in the Treasury.

Strong-boxes of the Treasury.

From the room of the Hadrianeum one cannot at the present pass through into the **Festoon Room**, so-called because of the decorative motifs in the frieze (painted by the same hand, and around the same time, as the decoration in the Hadrianeum). With its large ceiling decoration of a unicorn (the heraldic symbol of Paul III), this room is at present awaiting restoration, but it does contain the large canvas of *Cardinal Gozzadini receiving James III of England at Imola* which was painted in 1717–19 by Antonio Gionina, a pupil of Giuseppe Maria Crespi. The attribution and exact subject-matter are confirmed by a passage in Cesare Crespi's 1769 *Lives of the Bolognese Painters*. From here we return therefore to the Library, where a now closed doorway leads into the part of the building that is still occupied by the Italian Army; passing through it, one can go up a narrow corridor (with paintings by Perin del Vaga) that passes between the Hadrianeum and the Festoon Room to the so-called **Cagliostro Room**, which was the triple space

built in the sixteenth century to provide a second floor to Paul III's apartments but was latter transformed into a prison, with the windows looking out towards Prati being bricked in. It was in this relatively luxurious cell that the trickster Giuseppe Balsamo—better known as Count Cagliostro—was imprisoned in 1789 (hence the name). The large central room is flanked by two small side rooms which are known as the Dolphin or Salamander and the Stork Cabinets because of the Farnese heraldic devices on the ceilings; the genre scene and landscape frescoes are all the work of Luzio Luzi. Moving back down the stairs and corridor, and out through the door, one then proceeds towards the opposite wall, where one can see traces of the external walls built at the end of the fourteenth century for Boniface IX, in order to make the drum above the mausoleum proper into a square-sided storey. Passing through a doorway—once again decorated with the coat-of-arms of Paul III; he clearly did not want to be forgotten—one comes to the small vestibule that leads into the Treasury.

Treasury

This circular rooms stands directly over the Justice Chamber and originally formed a single space with the Rotunda Room above it; tests have revealed that the spherical vault of the present ceiling was probably constructed during the Middle Ages. If one opens the wooden cabinets—of which more will be said later—one can see the fine brickwork of the original Roman walls, complete with the holes for the marble facing that were also to be seen at the lower level. Originally, therefore, this was one single splendid space, a sort of inaccessible *templum*, that reached up towards the skies above the

A Magus in the Hands of the Inquisition

A mix of ingenuousness and imposture, genius and charlatanism, of mysticism and debauchery"—this is Giuseppe Balsamo a.k.a Count Cagliostro in the words of Roberto Gervaso, who since the 1970s has been engaged in detailed research into the most famous "magus" and magician of the eighteenth century; recently re-published, his biography of the man recounts all the story of a life that could have come out of a novel. From archive documents, court memoranda and published apologia we know that the Balsamo was a Palermo-born con-man, who even as a youth gave proof of his skill as a forger, and thereafter gave free rein to his criminal imagination in an attempt to achieve a social status

that would otherwise have been denied him. His first training came under the aegis of an alchemist who claimed to have found the Philosopher's Stone—as well as developing an unguent that could be used to re-attach severed limbs—and would take the young man on a voyage of discovery through the Greek Islands, Asia Minor and Egypt. A wild teller of tall stories, Balsamo would then live a vagabond life with his wife Lorenza, with periods of remarkable fortune alternating with long periods of poverty in which he had to fall back on inventive stop-gaps. Magician, medium and necromancer, he was also a leading light in the Free Masons (as Count Cagliostro) and would for ten years be the very idol

of Europe, until he fell victim to one of his own confidence tricks and was crushed by the Catholic Church, which he had rashly dared to challenge by founding his own "Egyptian Rite" Masonic Lodge in Rome itself. Denounced by his calculating wife, he was tried and condemned to death by the Inquisition on 7 April 1791. Having been arrested on 27 December 1789 he had initially be imprisoned in Castel Sant'Angelo, and even as early as 30 December the Holy Office postponed the trial offering this bizarre, almost comically offensive, assessment of Cagliostro: "a man who believes in nothing, who is without religion. In short, a vicious and most evil beast; he is

held to be a cheat, a raging and bestial charlatan, a rogue, an enthusiast, a most notorious deist…" But he would get away with it, pronouncing his abjuration of heresy in this very place, after which the pope commuted his sentence to life imprisonment and "salutary penitence," ordering that he be moved to the high security prison of San Leo. And that grim pile would be the final resting-place of a man who was the very incarnation of an Enlightenment which, for all its supposed "Rationalism," was still susceptible to the lure of the occult and spiritualism. But then our own disabused and jaundiced age is not above letting itself be duped, is it? (N.G.)

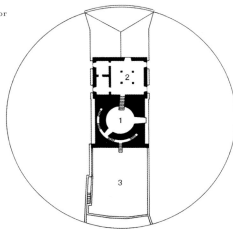

Plan of the sixth floor
of the Castle.

1. Rotunda
2. Column Room
3. Angel Terrace

building—and this is why some
scholars have argued it was the
actual burial chamber of the
emperor. D'Onofrio, for
example, pointed out the far
from coincidental similarities
between this space and
the Ravenna mausoleum
of Theodoricus, a king who
was particularly fascinated by
Hadrian's Mausoleum and wanted
his own burial chamber to be a
raised central-plan space, a sort
of unattainable ivory tower. The
circular nature of the original
space is still revealed by the
concentric rings of the terracotta
flooring, whilst the present
polygonal appearance dates from
1545, when Paul III had the
architectural-motif cabinets fitted
around the walls (the top of which
was already painted with a thin
cornice of plant volutes); these
were intended to house the papers
and land registers of the Papal
States, the *archivium arcis* which had
for safety reasons been moved to
the Castle some time before. It is
very rare to find sixteenth-century
furnishings still in the room for
which they were designed, and—
after recent restoration—one can
appreciate the full splendour of
the decoration: the in-lays of
Farnese fleur-de-lis on the
stepped panelling that links up to
the vault; the refined Doric frieze

of the faux architrave resting on
high-socle pilaster strips standing
between the moulded doors.
Another inlaid panel—placed as
an epigraph in the triumphal arch
of the monumental doorway—
once again commemorates Paul
III and the date that the
furnishings for the Treasury
were created. The room, in fact,
had been used to store precious
objects long before Sixtus V at the
end of the sixteenth century had a
large chest installed here to hold
millions of gold *scudi*—money
which the pontiff alone could use
and, even then, only after giving
full satisfaction that this was a case
of grievous need (for example,
a threat to the Papal States or to
Christendom itself). Later, this
like so many areas in the Castle
would become a prison: a still
legible inscription inside one
of the cabinet doors lists all the
historical novels of Sir Walter
Scott which had been devoured
by one particular prisoner in his
attempts to distract himself from
his plight, and another (again
nineteenth-century) inscription
was carved by a certain
"Bonaventura (sic!) Piacentini,
imprisoned by scum…"
Leaving the room, a narrow spiral
staircase dating from the Roman
period takes one up some thirty
or so steep steps to the doorway
of the Rotunda Room, on the
left. As has already been
mentioned, this occupies the top
room created when the tall space
of the upper chamber of the
imperial tomb was divided. (*N.G.*)

The Rotunda, the Column
Room and the Two Flag Rooms
For around ten years these rooms
housed the Castle's sculpture
collection, which is now
undergoing thorough restoration.
Given the importance of the
collection and the special nature
of its architectural surroundings,
the following aims nevertheless

o give a brief historic outline of the individual works and rooms that house them, in preparation for the completion of the restoration process.

The **Rotunda Room** at present contains some parts of Verschaffelt's bronze angel which were not replaced *in situ* after the restoration; these include the sword and sheath, as well as the iron and wood framework that once braced the eighteenth-century statue. The room also has the gilded wood *St. Michael* produced in 1736 by Pietro Bracci for the Leo X Chapel. Recently restored and cleaned, this has been returned to its original splendour: the painting and gilding have been revived and one can now appreciate the fine carving and elegance of a work whose late-Baroque style is typical of an artist who was most painstaking in the rendition of even the slightest detail. Bracci's *St. Michael* now takes its rightful place as one of the most important examples of eighteenth-century Roman sculpture.

A few steps bring one up to the **Column Room** and the two **Flag Rooms**, which have recently been identified as the three rooms built during the papacy of Benedict XIV as an extension to the Archive (at the time still housed in the Rotunda). Comparison of the present rooms with the 1749 plans reveals that they have remained unchanged except for the ceiling and the stairs linking them to the Rotunda. However, like elsewhere in the building, the old furnishings—the large cabinets of carved walnut with the coat-of-arms of Benedict XIV, the archivists' tables and desks, the wooden window surrounds—have been lost. The present appearance is the result of the decoration carried out in 1926 by the Roman artist Duilio Cambellotti.

The initial 1925 charter of the Castel Sant'Angelo Museum laid down that it was, amongst other things, to house some of the most important mementoes of the Italian Army, including the flags and colours of disbanded regiments. Headed by General Mariano Borgatti, the Management Committee decided to place these precious relics in the rooms once occupied by the Archives, which were thus to be decorated with motifs that reflected the achievements of the regiments. This work was commissioned from Cambellotti, whose completed decoration was approved by the museum Committee on 12 May 1926. In later years, the work however ran the risk of being destroyed; first because it was considered unsuitable to "the patriotic, almost religious, solemnity of the relics," and then because it was considered redundant after those mementoes had been moved to the Vittoriano monument. The decor's survival was due solely to bureaucratic sluggishness in dismantling it, and when the room was set up as the museum's Sculpture Gallery, the entire work was thoroughly restored. The decoration of the *Column*

Pietro Bracci, *St. Michael the Archangel*, 1736, carved wood gilded with goldleaf. Museo Nazionale di Castel Sant'Angelo.

View of the Column Room.

The Lament of the Dead Christ,
fifteenth century,
whole group and detail.
Museo Nazionale
di Castel Sant'Angelo
(photo A. De Luca).

Room—so named because of the columns supporting the ceiling—comprises both naturalistic motifs and *trompe-l'oeil*, the interweave of laurel branches (the classic symbol of victory) serving to create an illusion of depth in the low ceiling of the vault. As in the other rooms, the basic schema involves a jutting cornice decorated with symbols of war, and tempera decoration with more joyful motifs; these latter were closer to the personal aesthetics of the artist, who had never before undertaken a work inspired primarily by patriotic and military themes.

In the 1920s the Column Room housed the colours of various infantry regiments, whilst the next two rooms contained those of cavalry and commando units. The ceiling decoration reflects these differences: for example, in the **first Flag Room**, the stucco frieze contains groups of three horse heads above which are the various multi-coloured standards of the cavalry regiments; whilst in the **second Flag Room**, the cornice is decorated with intermingled arms brandishing a variety of weapons, and the tempera decoration depicts emblems and standards from various periods of Italian history (from the Roman *labarum* to the modern-day Italian flag). The works of sculpture housed here included the already-described bust of the *Salvator*

Mundi; the two busts from the niches of the Michelangelo facade on the Courtyard of Honour; the fourteenth-century well-head discovered during the building of the Trastevere station; the marble bust of Paul IV (Giovanni Pietro Carafa), part of the colossal statue by Vincenzo de' Rossi which had stood in the Campidoglio but then been hurled into the Tiber by the Romans; a *Franciscan Saint*, attributed to Jacopo della Quercia; a fine group sculpture in wood of *The Lament of the Dead Christ*; a terracotta *Pietà* and the marble tabernacle from the church of San Lorenzo in Lucina. The Flag Rooms contain depictions of Castel Sant'Angelo dating from various periods, including Francesco Aerni's painting of *The "Roman Candle" at the Castle*. (L.B.)

Continuing up the stairs one finally comes to the large **"Angel" Terrace** at the top of the mausoleum, so-called because it is dominated by the gigantic bronze Angel cast in Rome by the Flemish artist Pieter van Verschaffelt in 1752, and installed here on a plinth of travertine. In the space once occupied by the bronze quadriga atop the pagan mausoleum now stands *St. Michael the Archangel Sheathing his Sword*, which is only the last of the various sculptural representations here of the angelic figure who appeared to St. Gregory the Great in sign that the terrible plague God had inflicted on the city had come to an end. In 1497 a fire caused a barrel of gunpowder kept in the rooms below to explode, thus destroying the marble statue raised here by Nicholas V. This was immediately replaced by the Angel of Raffaello da Montelupo, which as we have seen fared only slightly better before being replaced by the present statue, fresh from a thorough recent

Tabernacle in polychrome
marble from the Roman
church of San Lorenzo in
Lucina, seventeenth century.
Museo Nazionale di Castel
Sant'Angelo
(photo A. De Luca).

Bronze angel by Pieter van
Verschaffelt, 1752, which
now stands on the top
of the Castle, detail
(photo A. De Luca).

restoration. As we saw in the
Rotunda Room, the complex
internal braces that held the
figure in place have now been
entirely renewed, so once again
this elegant, refined Angel can
spread its wings over the Castle,
its garments fluttering in the
wind.

Below the Angel, in the central
tower of the Castle, one can see
two carvings of coats-of arms.
The upper one is that of Paul III,
the lower of Alexander VI. Above
the Angel, to the left, is the
Campana della Misericordia [Mercy
Bell], so-called because it used
to toll at executions, commonly
held in the lowest courtyard of the
Castle (known as the Firing Squad
Courtyard). The bell itself dates
back to the middle of the
eighteenth century and replaces
an earlier one dating from the
papacy of Alexander VII (c. 1660)
that was damaged by one of the
'Roman Candles' that were
set up here to illuminate the
entire Castle. The terrace below

is known in documents as the
Breastplate or Trophy Terrace
because of the armour fixed at
intervals into the balustrade—they
figure in drawings as early as the
fifteenth century—and it provides
one of the most striking views
of Rome: a kaleidoscopic display
of Baroque cupolas, St. Peter's
and the palaces of the Vatican,
the hills of the Quirinale and
the Janiculum, and then beyond
them, the Castelli Romani,
the Prenestine hills and the
outline of Monte Soratte.
A different set of steps now
leads one down to the **Castle
Governor's Apartment**, which
is at present closed to the public
and awaiting re-organisation.
Comprising various rooms, it was
built above the Julius II Loggia
for Zenobio Savelli, Castle
Governor from 1730 to 1752;
access to it was by means of the
"lift" we have already seen.
Finally, one comes to the round
corridor built for Alexander VII
(1657), which runs alongside the

The Tabernacle from the Church of San Lorenzo in Lucina

Described in old
documents as "a cabinet
of fine marbles of
various colours, with
different seraphs and
festoons in gilded
bronze," the tabernacle
was once part of the
high altar of the church
of San Lorenzo in
Licina, backing onto a
large band of red marble
that served as the base
for Guido Reni's
painting of *The Crucifixion*.
It was removed during
the nineteenth century,
and has now been
replaced by a two-door
tabernacle in marble-
finish wood.
The high altar was
commisioned to make
a suitable setting
for Guido Reni's large
painting, and also
to serve as a tomb

of the man who had
donated that work
to the Friars Minor
of the church. The
overall design was by
Carlo Rainaldi, official
architect to the priests
of San Lorenzo, and
the work was installed
by 1676; the actual
carving was by
Pietro Antonio Ripoli,
a refined craftsman
who is also credited
with the railing and
floor of the altar.
Here again, restoration
has brought out
the high quality of the
worksmanship, which
makes this a very
valuable example
of the skill of
seventeenth-century
Roman craftsmen
working in marble.
(*L.B.*)

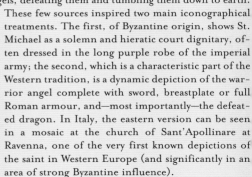

Unknown artist, *St. Michael the Archangel*, c. 1299, tempera on wood, Tretyakov Gallery, Moscow.

Veneration of St. Michael the Archangel was extraordinarily widespread in Europe during the Middle Ages, and from north to south there were a number of important sites of devotion dedicated to him: Mont Saint-Michel, the Sacra di San Michele in Val di Susa and the Monte Sant'Angelo in the Gargano. The cult of this archangel originated in the East, and so Puglia—thanks to its geographical position—became the first major centre for such devotion in Western Europe; by the end of the fourth century, it was already attracting thousands of pilgrims.

The sources for the iconography associated with St. Michael are primarily the Books of the Prophets and St. John's Book of Revelation. In the Book of Daniel, for example, St. Michael the Archangel appears alongside Gabriel as the defender of the Chosen People; in the Book of Joshua, he appears with drawn sword to the Jewish general during the siege of Jericho, declaring himself to be "the prince of the Lord's armies"; and, finally, in the Book of Revelation, he leads the celestial hosts against the dragon and the rebel angels, defeating them and tumbling them down to earth.

These few sources inspired two main iconographical treatments. The first, of Byzantine origin, shows St. Michael as a solemn and hieratic court dignitary, often dressed in the long purple robe of the imperial army; the second, which is a characteristic part of the Western tradition, is a dynamic depiction of the warrior angel complete with sword, breastplate or full Roman armour, and—most importantly—the defeated dragon. In Italy, the eastern version can be seen in a mosaic at the church of Sant'Apollinare at Ravenna, one of the very first known depictions of the saint in Western Europe (and significantly in an area of strong Byzantine influence).

The dynamic version is, however, much more common in Italy. Based on the story told in the Book of Revelation, this would become a firmly established part of religious iconography from the beginning of the sixteenth century onwards—thanks largely to the version painted by Raphael (now in the Louvre). Amongst the most significant variations on the theme one should perhaps mention that painted in 1635 by Guido Reni for the Church of the Capuchins in Rome. Here, as in the sixteenth-century sculpture within the grotto of Monte Sant'Angelo, St. Michael is shown wearing a Roman cuirass and a flowing cloak whilst he treads down upon a faun-eared devil, who lies chained to a metal "lead," one end of which is gripped in the angel's left hand.

Further features in the iconography of "St. Michael the Combatant" are due to the fact that in the early centuries of the Christian era it was not uncommon for ancient forms of pagan devotion to influence the cult of Christian saints. One such overlapping was that

Maestro di Castelsardo,
St. Michael the Archangel,
detail of the Tuili Retable,
1498–1500, tempera
on panel. St. Peter's Parish
Church, Tuili.

between St. Michael and Hermes/Mercury, who in pagan mythology was the god who led souls down to the underworld. Hence the idea of the Archangel as a supreme judge, complete with scales to weigh the virtues and vices of the deceased—an idea that was also inspired by a passage in the Letter of Jude in which Michael and Satan compete over possession of the body of Moses. Numerous representations of St. Michael in Castel Sant'Angelo have come down to us. First of all, as Marica Mercalli and Sergio Guarino have noted, there are the three sculptures: the marble statue created by Raffaello da Montelupo in 1544 (now in the Courtyard of Honour); the eighteenth-century gilded wood carving that original stood in the Leo X Chapel and is now in the Rotunda Room; and the splendid bronze statue installed on the roof terrace in 1752. The angel protector of the building also appears in the painted decoration of the Farnese apartments: Pellegrino Tibaldi painted a monumental version on the north wall of the Sala Paolina; Luzio Luzi did a fresco of the angel in the vault of the same room; Domenico Zaga painted him in the Justice Chamber; and finally an angel in painted stucco appears in the central rhomb of the Perseus Room ceiling. There are also those depictions of St. Michael which have been lost or were planned but never produced. These include the bronze group that Clement VII commissioned from Baccio Bandinelli to crown the tower of the Passetto di Borgo (all that remains is a preparatory drawing, now in the Louvre) and the seventeenth-

century cycle of frescoes with the *Story of St. Michael* in the Leo X Chapel (destroyed in the subsequent reworkings of the interior). All of these versions actually embody a slight modification of the traditional western iconography of "St. Michael the Combatant." The nuance here is rather different, resulting in an interpretation that is almost the very opposite of the more widespread depiction of the angel as a guardian of the Christian people. The association of the Angel and the mausoleum is linked to the legendary apparition of 590, when in re-sheathing his sword St. Michael decreed the end of the epidemic of the plague. Hence, in this case his weapon had not been turned against the devil, and the angel had not been acting as a protection against evil. He himself was the agent of God's wrath: the plague having been unleashed in punishment for the Romans' sins, St. Michael acted as the emissary who inflicted that terrible sentence. The numerous depictions of the archangel created for Castel Sant'Angelo might reveal a variety of techniques and styles, yet in each one of them what we see is a St. Michael who is not reassuring and protective but awesome and ruthless—an image that was perfectly in keeping with the fact that he was here associated with a place that was both fortress and prison. (*L.B.*)

Guido Reni, *St. Michael the Archangel*, 1635, oil on silk. The Capuchin Church of Santa Maria della Concezione, Rome.

Rogier van der Weyden, St. Michael the Archangel, detail from the *Last Judgement*, polyptych, 1445–50, oil on panel. Hôtel Dieu, Beaune.

Tosca Takes Her life in Protesting Her Love

This terrace overlooking the city is dear to opera-lovers because it is the setting of the last scene in one of Puccini's most popular works, *Tosca*. The passionate woman has come to the Castle where her lover, Mario Cavaradossi, a painter first met in the church of Sant'Andrea della Valle, is about to be executed. Having killed the brutal chief of police, Scarpia, in Palazzo Farnese, Tosca is convinced that she has saved her lover, that the execution is just going to be a fake. However, when she realises the truth, she throws herself off the parapet in despair. Castel Sant'Angelo has been re-created thousands of times on the world's stages, but in a recent television production of the opera, shot at the actual sites at the actual times mentioned in the libretto, one finally got to see that terrible dawn here, with the massive cupola of St. Peter's in the background. (*N.G.*)

One of the finest views in Rome, laid before an angel so intent on what he is doing he doesn't seem to notice it.

Julius II Loggia to create some sort of symmetry between this side and the other side of the drum, with the Pius IV Loggia. On one's left is a staircase that now brings one to the most prestigious of all the Farnese apartments in Castel Sant'Angelo, the Sala Paolina. (*N.G.*)

Sala Paolina

This was the room in which the pope received delegations during his periods of residence in the Castle; and here, in the space most easily accessible to visitors, that celebration of the person and political figure of Alessandro Farnese which we have already seen in the decoration of the Library reached its high point. So, once again, one must look not only at the magnificence of the paintings and frescoes, which strike us just as powerfully as any sixteenth-century visitor, but also at the message that the pope and his court intended to convey. The iconography here seems to solemnise the very apotheosis of Paul III, who is presented as the link between two apparently irreconcilable worlds: that of pagan Antiquity and that of Christianity. The schema in the Sala Paolina is much more complete and coherent than that in the Library, decorated just a few years earlier, and the works are an expression of the full magnificence of this Renaissance pontiff, who here underlines that the legitimacy of his own spiritual and temporal authority rests on a historical continuity between

the Roman Empire and the Universal Catholic Church. The Sala Paolina stands in the southern part of the Farnese apartments, and documentary evidence indicates it was decorated from 1545 onwards: to be more precise, the frescoes in this room were painted between June 1545 and

September 1547, and registers of payment—together with a number of extant preparatory drawings—confirm that this celebration of papal power was the work of Perin del Vaga. Documentary sources do not tell us, however, why Paul III dismissed Luzio Luzi as the artist in charge of the Castel Sant'Angelo decoration, though it could well be that he simply saw that the higher quality of Perin's work was more likely to guarantee the success of this all-important second phase of the project. And, in effect, what the Tuscan has produced here is a visual "apparatus" that is as perfect in execution and style as it is complex in iconography, with traditional decorative motifs being re-worked in new and original ways. The painted decoration seems to present us with an illusionistic architectural space superimposed upon the real space of the room, with fake columns and niches surmounted by a fake architrave. This architectural framework enables the artist to combine all the elements of the composition in an ordered and organic whole; at the same time, it gives him the opportunity to demonstrate all his skill in the creation of a grandiose visual illusion that was so in keeping with the Mannerist delight in plays upon the ambiguity of reality and appearance. What is more, when designing the decoration of this room, Perin del Vaga decided to invert the classic proportions between decoration and narration. Proceeding in a manner that was the very opposite of what we saw downstairs in the Library, he made the decorative motifs and figures monumental and reduced the size of the narrative scenes, which no longer dominate a background of grotesques. The approach developed

in the decoration of this room would prove to be a model for all large-scale decorative projects in Rome during the second half of the sixteenth century.

The ceiling is a cavetto vault, a form of barrel vault much appreciated by Mannerist architects because the truncation of the usual rounded vaulting provides a large central panel for decoration. Here again we can see the coat-of-arms of Paul III, the leitmotif of the entire decorative schema. As one looks upwards, one is dazzled by the very brightness of the decoration, with the dominant colours of the stucco-work and grotesque-motif friezes being gold and white; the result is therefore to create an illusion of even greater space. Within the central frame, the Farnese crest is flanked symmetrically by two ovals in stucco-work that are decorated with the mythological scenes of *The Triumph of Galatea* (towards the south wall, from where one goes out into the Julius II Loggia) and a *Procession of Marine Animals* (towards the north). East and west of the crest is this celebratory phrase in Greek: "Paul III, Pontifex Maximus, has transformed the tomb of the Great Hadrian into a mighty and sacred abode."

Plan of the fourth floor of the Castle.

1. Covered Walkway (archaeological gallery)
2. Pius IV Rooms
3. Julius II Loggia
4. Sala Paolina
5. Perseus Room
6. Room of Cupid and Psyche
7. Paul III Loggia
8. Uncovered Walkway
9. Armoury

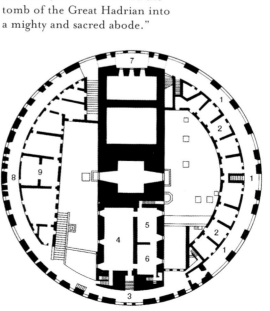

QVAE OLIM INTRA HANC ARCEM COLLAPSA

This entire central section is then enclosed within a wider frame of stucco-work and grotesques, which extends to the curved edges of the vault. Here the decoration includes scenes from the Life of Alexander the Great: *Alexander Encountering the High Priest at the Gates of Jerusalem* (north side), *Alexander Praying in the Temple of Jerusalem* and *Alexander Burning the Booty to Lighten the Load in his Wagons* (over the east wall, which leads into the Cupid and Psyche Room); *Porus Attacked by the Macedonian Soldiers* (south side); *Alexander Having Ships Built to Cross the Hydaspes* and *Alexander's Triumphal Entry into Babylonia* (west side). The reference was both a play on the pontiff's own Christian name and a reminder of his love of Classical culture. What is more, it offered further proof of Paul III's admiration for Hadrian, who had himself been a great admirer of Alexander's cultural eclecticism. However, the decoration of the Sala Paolina does not only highlight the link between the political projects of Alexander the Great, Hadrian and Paul III; it also emphasises a cultural affinity: Greek, the language of Alexander, was the chosen language of Hadrian and—in a demonstration of his own cultured humanism— was that used by Paolo Farnese in the ceiling inscription that celebrates his own work on the imperial tomb.

The ceiling decoration is completed by stucco-work motifs that take up devices connected with the Farnese family: in the four corners are the fleur-de-lis accompanied by the Greek motto *Dikes krinon* (Lily of Justice) and the dolphin with the Augustan motto, *Festina lente* (Make Haste Slowly). The two longer sides of the vault curve also bear the coat-of-arms of Mario Ruffini, the Castle Governor.

Then comes the frieze decorating the architrave, which has a Latin

The Sala Paolina
(photo A. De Luca).

The Sala Paolina, detail of the pendentive with the motto "Festina lente" [Make Haste Slowly], stucco.

inscription in gold lettering, again celebrating Paul III's work on the Castle: "All that within this castle was once decayed, defaced and inaccessible, now through the merits of the pontiff Paul III one sees restored, set in order and decorated to meet the needs of stout solidity, comfortable utility and fine elegance."

As has already been mentioned, the walls are decorated with painted columns resting on a painted socle; this latter is decorated with frescoed panels of *Battles between Sea Creatures*, which are separated by hermaphrodite caryatids. Between the columns are painted niches, decorated with representations of the *Cardinal Virtues*, and large monochrome panels painted to look like bronze alto-relievi (again depicting episodes from the Life of Alexander the Great). Above the side doors, some of them trompe l'oeil, are couples of allegorical figures with tondi that illustrate episodes from the *Life of St. Paul*, the saint whose name was taken by this Farnese pontiff; again this conjunction of the Christian and the Classical serves to underline that the pope was both a temporal

and spiritual power.
Between the painted columns
bearing the fake architrave over
the north wall stands the splendid
monumental *St. Michael the Archangel*
painted by the young Pellegrino
Tibaldi under the direct guidance
of Perin del Vaga.
The doorway to the left leads
into the **Pompeii Corridor** and
is surmounted by a sopraporta
decorated with allegories of *Faith*
and *Religion*; above this is a tondo
of *The Conversion of St. Paul*. The
doorway to the right, with its two
servants, is simply a trompe l'oeil
creation (during the restoration
organised by Mariano Borgatti,
part of the painting was removed,
revealing the original Roman
brickwork beneath). Above this
fake doorway there are allegories
of *Church* and *Concord*, on which
rests a tondo of *St. Paul Preaching
to the Jews*. On the socles, the very
life-like figures of the two baboons
are seen against the fresco
of the *Battle of the Sea Creatures*.

Perin del Vaga and his Circle

As he began work of the last phase of his apartments in the Castle, Paul III was determined to employ the services of an artist of proven skill, who would guarantee that the decoration of the most prestigious rooms in the palace would be suitably grandiose and spectacular. In fact, the work required someone capable not only of designing an entire cycle of frescoes, but also of overseeing their production by all the various artists that were to be involved in completing the project. In 1545, therefore, he appointed one man to take charge of all the work in the south wing of the new apartments—the Sala Paolina, the Perseus Room and the Cupid and Psyche Room. His choice fell upon the Florentine artist Perin del Vaga, who—with the death of Raphael, the flight of artists resulting from the Sack of Rome, and Michelangelo's as yet unfinished work on the Sistine Chapel—proved to be the one suitable candidate for the job. Perin del Vaga had already had experience working on the decoration of such imposingly "public" spaces, even if in the relative "backwater" of Genoa; what is more, he was capable of combining the great lessons taught by Raphael and Michelangelo with that rich repertoire of decorative motifs and ideas that had emerged in the Roman Mannerism of these years (a style that was certainly dear to the pontiff himself, and to those whom the decoration of Castel Sant'Angelo was intended to impress). Finally, one undoubted point in the artist's favour was his proven ability in organising large-scale projects. In effect, these rooms present the modern-day visitor with a unique opportunity to appreciate something of the working methods applied in such Renaissance projects, which involved one maestro, responsible for overall design and organisation, and a number of specialised craftsmen and artists. Perin del Vaga's own managerial capacities would soon become clear to his contemporaries, working in conditions that Vasari describes in these terms: "always a hundred things on his mind, and surrounded by sculptors, stucco-workers, carvers, dress-makers, embroiderers, painters, gilders and other similar craftsmen, he never got an hour's rest." And the central role he played in the entire scheme is borne out by the fact that almost all the contracts and bills of payment for each part of the decoration bear only his name (with the exception of Marco Pino, who is credited with the frescoes of the *Episodes from the Life of Alexander the Great* in the vault of the Sala Paolina). However, stylistic analysis of the decoration, reveals that the squad at work did not only involve the craftsmen mentioned by Vasari but also a number of painters, responsible for decorating the walls to designs drawn up by the maestro. Along with Marco Pino, these included Gerolamo Siciolante, who painted the monumental portrait of Hadrian on the south wall of the Sala Paolina, Domenico Zaga, Michele da Lucca, Livio Agresti and even Pellegrino Tibaldi, who in later decades would become one of the leading architects and artists of Late Mannerism. This latter painter is credited with the monumental angel in the Sala Paolina, a work in which one can clearly see that the young man (he had been born in Como in 1527) was already striving to achieve a certain independence of expression within the confines of the rigorous control exerted by Perin del Vaga. (L.B.)

In the east wall there are another two doorways: one real, leading through into the Perseus Room, the other trompe l'oeil (the painted figure of the sculptor with his tools has never been satisfactorily identified by scholars). The allegories above the doorways are of Classical inspiration, comprising two pairs of Muses, whilst the tondi show *St. Paul Preaching to the Pagans* and *The Blinding of Elymus*, and the fake niches contain allegories of *Temperance* and *Prudence*. The three frescoed panels of alto-relievo in monochrome show other events from the life of Alexander the Great: *Alexander Placing the Poems of Homer in a Casket*; *Alexander Cuts the Gordian Knot*; *Alexander Spares the Family of Darius*.

In the south wall both doorways are real: one leading to the Julius II Loggia (surmounted by allegories of *Charity* and *Abundance*, with a tondo of *The Sacrifice of Lystra*), the other to the Castle Governor's Apartments (surmounted by *Hope* and *Celestial Venus*, with a tondo of *The Martyrdom of St. Paul*). In the space between the columns appears the figure the pope seems to have taken as his tutelary spirit, the emperor Hadrian. Painted here by Gerolamo Siciolante, the figure is shown as it might appear in official portraits of the second century AD: over a long white tunic, the emperor wears the uniform of a general, comprising a cuirass decorated with mascherons, a cloak, richly-adorned sandals

Perin del Vaga and assistants, *The Two Servants*, fresco (detail). Sala Paolina.

preceding pages
Marco Pino, *Porus Attacked by Macedonian Soldiers*, fresco (detail). Sala Paolina (photo A. De Luca).

Perin del Vaga and assistants, *Alexander has the Poems of Homer Placed in a Chest*, fresco. Sala Paolina.

Perin del Vaga and assistants, *The Martyrdom of St. Paul* and a *sopraporta* with *Hope* and *The Celestial Venus*, fresco. Sala Paolina.

and a sword. The features are based on those shown in original portraits: curly hair, a thick beard and eyes slightly close together. On the west wall are three windows, in the upper embrasure of which are again frescoes of scenes from the Life of Alexander the Great: from left to right, *Group of Soldiers Warming Themselves*

at a Fire; *An Old Man Presenting Alexander with the Model of a Boat*; *Alexander Receiving the Wreath of Victory*. The fake niches contain allegories of *Strength* and *Justice*, whilst the monochrome alto-relievi show *Alexander Resolving a Quarrel between Two Fellow Soldiers* and *Alexander Raising Twelve Altars to Commemorate his Victories in India*. (L.B.)

The Pompeii Corridor

A winding, low corridor links the two main rooms of the Farnese apartments (the Library and the Sala Paolina), and its meanders reveal that it is of Roman origin: it must have been a slightly-sloping gallery leading up to the top levels of the tower. Nowadays it is known as the Pompeii Corridor because of the style of the precious paintings that decorate its entire length, lit by small regularly-spaced rectangular windows that we have already seen from the courtyard below. Protected behind sheets of glass, this decoration is a fine example of those grotesque motifs inspired by the Classical art which was being rediscovered at the end of the fifteenth century (especially in the recently-excavated Domus Aurea; the name "grotesque" in fact comes from the fact that such motifs were first discovered in grottoes). It was Raphael, appointed Prefect for the Antiquities of Rome, and (even more so) the school of his followers who would exploit the full splendour of such decoration, combining heraldic, naturalistic and mythological motifs to create elaborate and erudite schemes of adornment for Renaissance palaces both inside and outside Italy. Perin del Vaga and his workshop, who were responsible for this work in the Pompeii Corridor, stayed substantially true to the example set by Raphael, their designs and

palette remaining largely faithful to the examples discovered through antiquarian research (even if the usual black, white and red are here combined with a more "impressionistic" use of yellow and green).

Perseus Room

Moving back into the Sala Paolina, one now goes through into the two rooms that were probably intended as the pontiff's private apartments. Their names come from the main figures in the mythological scenes in the frescoed friezes along the top of the walls, which were painted between 1545 and 1547 to original designs by Perin del Vaga. Hence, the first of them is the Perseus Room, the figure of that mythological hero appearing in a wooden sculpture at the centre of a ceiling of erudite grotesque motifs against a blue background enclosed within a heavy gold frame that is, inevitably, decorated with Farnese devices and mottoes (one cannot help finding the shocking pink used to render the flesh of the carved figure rather kitsch). The actual myth of the Greek hero is skilfully recounted in six double or triple panels that unfolded amidst a framework comprising gleaming white unicorns caressed by elegant ladies and a veritable explosion of drapery-holding putti on an excessively narrow cornice from which hang festoons of flowers and fruit linked by tragic masks. The story starts on the shorter wall to the left as one enters (the small door in the wall gives onto a short staircase Paul III had created within the Roman walls to give him direct access to the Clement VII Bathhouse). The first scene in the narrative shows this Son of Zeus taking his leave of king Polydectes, who had received him on the island of Seriphos (in the Cyclades) after the boy and his

preceding pages
Two Baboons, fresco.
Sala Paolina
(photo A. De Luca).

Gerolamo Siciolante,
The Emperor Hadrian, fresco.
Sala Paolina.

Comparison of the decoration in the Pompeii Corridor and that to be seen on the walls of corridor n. 79 in the Domus Aurea reveals just how much the former drew on the latter.

mother Danae had been cast into the sea in a wooden chest. To this adoptive father, the young man promises to bring the head of Medusa, one of the terrible Gorgons—or, perhaps, as another version of the myth has it, he is forced to do so by a king intent on seducing Danae in his absence. In the painting we can see two of the deities who assisted Perseus in his task: Athena, who gives him a magic mirror, and Hermes, who gives him winged sandals and a sharp, steel bill-hook. On the wall alongside are two scenes cut by the large windows (which were probably modified after the completion of the decoration): in the embrasure the decor shows Apollo firing an arrow at a winged monster; Apollo and Daphne and the river Peneus; Perseus questioning the Graeae about the whereabouts of the Gorgons (perhaps the sisters of these monstrous virgins who, born already old, lived in the Valley of the Phorcides) and then proceeding upon his way having obtained the information he requires. In the next panel,

by which one entered, Perseus reaches the shore of Ethiopia where he sees the virgin Andromeda chained to a rock; the punishment is an expiation for the rash words of her mother, Cassiopia, who had dared to vaunt her own beauty over that of the Nereids. Seeing the young girl threatened by a sea monster, the hero falls in love with her and promises her father, the king of that land, that he will rescue her if he can have her hand in marriage. The deal is struck, Perseus flies up into the air (thanks to his winged sandals) and effortlessly dispatches the monster conjured up by Poseidon to avenge the Nereids. In the last scene, over the door, the hero returns to the island of Seriphos where he learns that Polydectes has taken his mother by force. For this he takes a terrible revenge: the severed head of Medusa is still in his possession—the dripping blood is said to be the origin of coral—and holding it up to the face of the tyrant the hero turns him into a statue of stone. And then, the happy ending: the marriage feast of Perseus and Andromeda. (*N.G.*)

The Perseus Room is one of those that best represents the criteria applied when the Castel Sant'Angelo Museum was first created. This was the time when numerous rooms of the Castle were filled with material of various provenance and date in order to recreate the atmosphere of the pope's private apartments, and although—as has already been said—from a scholarly point of view such an approach is hardly admissible today, the present-day curators of the museum have maintained this lay-out because it itself has become an important historical record of an earlier attitude to museum-design. Hence the fact that the Perseus Room contains tapestries,

Perseus surprises the sleeping Medusa—the only Gorgon to have remained mortal—and cuts off her head; he can then escape on the winged horse Pegasus, which emerges from the severed trunk of the slaughtered monster, as he is now invisible to the other two Gorgons thanks to helmet of Hades. Finally, back at the wall

a lectern, a prie-dieu, two chests and two paintings: Paris Bordon's *Christ Bearing the Cross* and a *Lament of the Dead Christ* by a painter of the Ferrara School. The *Christ Bearing the Cross* comes from the Menotti Collection and can be dated around 1550, during the full maturity of the Treviso-born artist, who had initially trained in the studios of Giorgione and Titian and then moved towards a much more Mannerist style influenced by the example of Pordenone and Lorenzo Lotto. Like this latter, Bordon would gain a large number of commissions outside Venice, in the eastern areas of Lombardy and, outside Italy, in places like Augsburg and Fontainbleau. His Venetian background is, however, clear in the Castel Sant'Angelo picture thanks to the evident delight he takes in the very handling of the paint, using colour to create a richly-luminous atmosphere that makes the end result very different from the treatments of the same theme by Giampietrino and Sebastiano del Piombo (which can also be seen in this museum).

On the wall opposite hangs the *Lady with a Unicorn*, which was part of the 1916 Menotti donation to Castel Sant'Angelo. Attributed to the Ravenna artist Luca Longhi (c. 1507–1580), the picture shows a young woman seated next to a unicorn, the symbol of purity and chastity that became one of the emblems adopted by the Farnese. Longhi, in fact, would work for that aristocratic family various times, and given the presence of the dynastic symbol in this painting, it seems highly likely that this is one of the works they commissioned from him: in fact, according to the most recent studies, it is probably a portrait of Giulia Farnese, sister of the future Pope Paul III, official mistress to the Borgia pope Alexander VI, and a very skilful promoter of the family's dynastic fortunes. The work reveals the artist's natural inclination for gentle and graceful forms, a characteristic of the "school" of Raphael as it developed in the Bologna and Romagna areas. The artist's association with those circles is also suggested by the classical beauty of the woman and the intense rendition of the landscape—all of which are compatible with an attribution to Longhi and a date of around 1535–40, that is around ten years after the death of Giulia Farnese. This could, therefore, be a posthumous portrait commissioned by a member of her family who was anxious to commemorate his relative and ennoble her memory by associating her with this symbol of purity. (*L.B.*)

The Cupid and Psyche Room
Too often visible solely through a wrought-iron gate across the doorway, this room contains a very well-preserved frieze of the famous story of Cupid and Psyche, which was so dear to the pupils of Raphael (one need only think of the remarkable version that appears in Giulio Romano's decorations of the Palazzo Te in Mantua). Perin del Vaga probably painted these frescoes himself, abandoning the use of grotesque-motif designs for a division of the tale into different panels separated by painted architectural and sculptural features. The story was such a popular tale that one can almost hear it being told by the old woman servant of the brigands who appears in the first panel after the entrance; the ass accompanying her is an erudite reference to Apuleius' *The Golden Ass* (or the *Metamorphosis*), the most complete written source for the tale. Psyche is named after the

Pompeii Corridor, detail of the wall decoration. The fanciful mixture of human, animal and plant forms within the architectural framework sometimes becomes positively "grotesque."

Perseus Room, the wooden
alto-relievo of Perseus
in the centre of the ceiling.

Perseus Room, detail
of the frieze with ladies
and unicorns
(photo A. De Luca).

human spirit, and in Roman painting she appears as a gentle beauty with the multicoloured wings of a butterfly (in popular myths, the soul was often represented as a butterfly that flutters away from the body after death). Here, however, she appears as she is described in the story, a girl whose beauty is so intimidating that it frightens all her suitors; whilst all her sisters are married, Psyche is yet to find a husband. In the scene above the door we see her desperate father consult an oracle, from whom he receives a terrible response: the sovereign is told that he must dress his daughter as if for marriage and then abandon her on a solitary rock where a horrible monster will appear to take possession of her. This is the plot which Venus, jealous

of the girl's beauty, has hatched, working in cahoots with her son, Cupid. But once this latter sees Psyche he falls hopelessly in love with her, and so as to avoid arousing the wrath of his mother, he has her carried away by the gentle west wind, Zephyrus, who raises her gently into the air and then sets her back onto the ground within an enchanted vale. In the angled architrave of the window one sees Psyche, exhausted by her emotional ordeal, fall asleep on a bed of soft grass. When she is awoken by the sound of music she is amazed to find herself in the flower-strewn garden of a marble palace. Entering the building, she is guided by voices that reveal to her that they are slaves at her service. At night, Cupid arrives and slips into her bed, where they pass the time joyously together. However there is one clear warning: she will never be allowed to see him; and if she does, she will lose him forever. After a while the girl begins to feel homesick for her family and lament that her poor father must think that she is dead; what is more, she is dying to tell her sisters all about what has happened to her. Cupid thus grants her wish; but the sisters, green with envy at Psyche's good fortune, convince her that her lover might be a monster and that she must discover the truth. At this point the girl cannot contain her curiosity, and on night she takes to bed with her an oil-lamp to discover the truth, and a razor to kill the monster (if that is what he turns out to be). However, to her delight and wonder, she finds that the person sleeping alongside her is a beautiful youth, and her hand shakes so much as she raises the lamp to see better that a drop of hot oil falls onto Cupid, who walks up and, as he had warned, is thus obliged to abandon her forever. This key episode, so rich

in pathos, is that painted directly opposite the doorway. Then comes Venus's scolding of her wayward son, whilst Ceres and Juno show some sympathy and understanding for Psyche, the young girl who is now distraught as she searches the world in vain for her love. She pleads with both Juno and then Venus, who relents slightly but imposes some very harsh penance on the girl:

amongst the other trials she has to undergo is a descent into the Underworld, where Pysche is to fill an urn with the water of youth that is guarded by Proserpina. However, on the way back she opens the amphora—in spite of the fact that she was forbidden to do so—and as a result falls into a deep sleep; yet Cupid, who has never forgotten his beloved, flies down to wake her with the prick

Perseus Room, *Perseus Killing Medusa* and the *Birth of Pegasus* (detail of the frieze).

of one of his arrows, then hurries back to Olympus to beseech Jove for permission to marry a mortal. The whole story thus ends happily with a magnificent wedding-banquet offered by the gods, where Psyche obtains her mother-in-law's blessing and thus achieves immortality. (*N.G.*)

The furnishings in this room too reflect the "atmospheric" criteria adopted by the first director of the museum, who turned this into a sort of papal bedroom with material of various provenance. Against the right wall is a bed, a wooden prie-dieu with a carved female figure, a small painted altar and a chest, together with Sebastiano del Piombo's *Christ Bearing the Cross*. From right to left on the wall facing the entrance is a *Portrait of Paul III*, a delightful spinet painted with grotesques and allegorical figures (the work of a mid-sixteenth-century artist from Emilia), a seventeenth-century copy of Federico Barocci's *Rest on the Flight into Egypt* and a *Portrait of Alexander VI*. On the left-hand wall are two chests and a *Pietà* by a sixteenth-century Brescian artist.

Part of the Contini Bonacossi donation, the Sebastiano del Piombo picture is dated by scholars to the very last years of the artist's life (1485–1547). Called to Rome in 1511, to work with Raphael on the decoration of Agostino Chigi's Villa Farnesina, Sebastiano del Piombo would obtain great success in the city,

and in 1531 was appointed to the lucrative position of *piombatore* [lead sealer] of papal breves and bulls (hence his name). Exposure to the work of Raphael and Michelangelo led him to combine close attention to the modelling of the human body (a feature of the painting of the Roman Renaissance) with that interest in the handling of light and colour which was characteristic of Venice (the city in which he had started his career); the result was a very original synthesis of these two very different approaches to painting. In his various returns to this theme of *Christ Bearing the Cross*, the artist intensified this development in his art, using ever grimmer and deader colours in an attempt to accentuate the expressive intensity and dramatic effect of the composition. With its distant gleams of light, the background landscape in the Castel Sant'Angelo painting is clearly inspired by his Venetian past, whilst the imposing figure in the foreground, a Christ whose ample vestments seem somehow to magnify him, is clearly influenced by the masters of Central Italy. Having left the Paul III apartments one now continues outside, around the top of the Castle, along the walkways created for the Borgia pope Alexander VI and then modified by various of his successors during the sixteenth and seventeenth centuries. The route we will follow is only one of many, given the complexity

Perseus Room, *Perseus
Killing the Sea Monster to Rescue
Andromeda and then Take her
Hand in Marriage,*
detail of the frieze.

Perseus Room, details
of the furnishings.

of the links between the spaces
within the building, and starts
anti-clockwise from the Julius II
Loggia (on the southern side
of the fortress) to then pass east
along the so-called Covered Walk
to end at the north in the loggia
built for Paul III. From this
height one has a fine view of the
fortress's defences: the polygonal
bastions around the square
walls, the Passetto di Borgo
extending from the San Marco
Bastion up towards the Vatican,
the pentagonal walls built for
Pius IV and the old moat of the
Castle. Julius II's intention when
he had this loggia built on the
Tiber side of the Castle in 1505
was to lighten the appearance
of the fortress and give it the
elegance befitting a princely

residence. Around forty years
later, Paul III would link up this
existing structure to his own Sala
Paolina: from this, the most
important room in the Pauline
apartments, a staircase leads down
to the terrace of the loggia, from
where one get an extraordinary
view of the Tiber and the Ponte
Sant'Angelo.
A bitter enemy of Alexander VI,
Giuliano della Rovere (the future
Julius II) was forced to leave
Rome during his papacy, and
when he himself was elected
pontiff he did everything in his
power to persecute the Borgias:
the entire family was
excommunicated and Cesare
Borgia—known as Il Valentino—
was actually imprisoned in
Castel Sant'Angelo before being

sent to Spain. Nephew of Sixtus IV, Julius II continued his uncle's programme of *renovatio urbis*, which was intended to make Rome the architectural expression of the universal power of the Church and the absolute power of the Papacy. This programme involved not only the re-structuring of the Vatican palaces but also the re-building of St. Peter's; however, amongst these mammoth undertakings, he did find time for Castel Sant'Angelo, appointing his favourite architect Giuliano da Sangallo to oversee the work here.

The fortifications within the heart of the Castle that had been built for Alexander VI were considered sufficient to guarantee the safety of the Curia in case of attack, so Julius II turned his attention to the accommodation within the Castle, modernising the apartments built for Nicholas V and, wherever possible, adapting the fortress to meet the high standards of his own refined taste. The scholars assume, therefore, that it was Guiliano da Sangallo who was commissioned to build this elegant loggietta, which replaced an old balcony and created a certain decorative relief in the solid mass of the keep. The loggia architrave rests on two thin columns whose capitals are decorated with heraldic motifs. The vaulting is also adorned with decorative friezes of grotesque motifs and three coats-of-arms in stucco; the one in the centre is that of Julius II.

Leaving this terrace and proceeding leftwards, one enters a gallery that runs around the eastern crown of the Castle. This is the so-called **Covered Walkway**; built at the behest of the Medici pope Pius IV in 1555–59, it involved the partial covering of the circuit around the Castle constructed for the Borgia pope at the end of the fifteenth

century. Through the arches cut into the walls one gets a splendid view of the Tiber overlooked by the San Giovanni and San Luca Bastions and part of the polygonal walls built for Pius IV. The spaces between the arched openings house the material that makes up the Castel Sant'Angelo **Archaeological Gallery**. The wall that supports the vaulting of the Covered Walkway was built for the Medici pope by modifying the small semicircular building that marked the southern end of the Theatre Courtyard (a second storey was added to it). Initially this space was used as facilities

Luca Longhi, *Lady with a Unicorn*, second quarter of the sixteenth century, oil on panel. Perseus Room (formerly in the Cupid and Psyche Room).

Cupid and Psyche Room.

Perin del Vaga, *The Brigands' Servant-Woman Tells Carites the Fable of Cupid and Psyche*. The ancient ruins create an atmosphere of melancholy nostalgia.

Psyche wakens Cupid, fresco.
Room of Cupid and Psyche.

Exterior view of the Julius II
Loggia that opens in the
cylindrical block of the
Castle,

The view of the Tiber
and the Ponte Sant'Angelo
from the Julius II Loggia.

for the artillery located on
the top of the Castle, and then
later transformed into "luxury"
cells for prisoners of a certain
importance. The two-storey
front onto the Theatre Courtyard
that was created by this work
was subsequently decorated with
frescoes of friezes and allegorical
figures (which have already been
described).
From the Covered Walkway one
comes into the Paul III Loggia
which was finished in 1543; this is
the date given on the plaque raised
in the central lunette by the Castle
Governor, Tiberio Crispo.
This belvedere has five arches
resting on pilasters and in
contemporary documents is
referred to as "the loggia looking
towards Prati." Originally there
was a second floor of an architrave
resting on columns, but this was
bricked in (at the command
of Paul III himself) to create what

are now known as the Cagliostro
Room and the Dolphin and Stork
Cabinets. The loggia, which opens
into an atrium leading to the
Festoon Room, was the work
of Raffaello da Montelupo.
The decoration, carried out
immediately after completion of
the structure (1543–44), was the
work of Gerolamo Siciolante da
Sermoneta, one of the most active
of those who worked under Perin
del Vaga on the decoration of the
Farnese apartments. As in the
southern loggia, here too exposure
to the elements and city smog have
not helped the preservation of the
frescoes, of which only parts are
still clearly legible. However,
what survive makes it clear that
the architectural link between
the papal apartments and
the belvedere was reflected in the
decorative schema, which again
continued the iconography used
in the Library and Hadrianeum.

Once again, the leitmotif is the parallel between Paul III and the emperor Hadrian, whose mausoleum has become the fortified residence of papal power. As has already been mentioned, Paul III—a man of great learning, with a humanist veneration for the art and history of Classical Antiquity—was a great admirer of Hadrian's political stature and cultural eclecticism. And as scholars confirm, like a perfect Renaissance prince, the pontiff had fully assimilated the lessons to be learnt from Roman emperors as to the propaganda uses of art and architecture. Just as in the fourth century AD Hadrian had promoted extensive building work in order to transform Rome into a symbol of his own power, so this "new Hadrian" aimed to impress his mark on the city. And, in the political sphere, he too felt the need to strengthen his borders— but this time not against barbarians but against Lutheran heresy, the expansionism of nascent European states and the threat posed by the Muslim empire. As we have seen, these parallels are elaborated upon in the decoration of the Paul III apartments, whilst here in the loggia restricted space allows for the depiction of only a few episodes and symbolic images. Nevertheless, there is enough

to remind the visitor that this pontiff is a worthy successor to Hadrian.

In the surviving pendentive is the scene of *Hadrian Burning the Promissory Notes Signed by the Roman People*, an act of imperial clemency imitated by Paul III at the moment of his election. The two lunettes contain imaginary reconstructions of ancient buildings. The first is a semi-circular colonnade in which the emperor seems to be giving a public audience; the very strange-looking building alongside bears a very worn plaque, but the inscription *ossa viri magni* (the remains of illustrious ancestors) suggest it is intended to be a sepulchre. The second image seems to be a fanciful version of

The Paul III Loggia (detail).

Colossal Portrait Bust of Antoninus Pius, mid second century AD. Museo Nazionale di Castel Sant'Angelo.

The Archaeological Gallery

Protected from the elements by large sheets of glass and illuminated by diffuse natural light, the display comprises various architectural and sculptural fragments from Hadrian's Mausoleum. Recently cleaned, the fragments of the moulded cornices with alto-relievo friezes of bucrania and sacrificial instruments—together

with a small Corinthian-style capital—were all part of the original decoration of the mausoleum. There is also a large *Head of Hadrian*, which probably comes from the mausoleum and is to be identified with that given in exchange for the larger and finer bust now to be seen in the Rotunda of the Vatican Museum (it has the

same treatment of the hair, with separate curls on the forehead, raised slightly at the temples). Extensively re-worked, this bust shows the emperor as a mature adult, illustrating a type of official iconography that continued to be used after his death. Quite apart from the fact that it is in the same type of Eastern Greek marble, various features

in the handling—the massive neck, the heavy brow and eyelids, the slight eyebrows, and the different treatment of the moustache and the beard—link it with the *Colossal Portrait Bust of Antoninus Pius*, also found at the mausoleum. It was this latter emperor who would complete the work on Hadrian's monumental tomb. (*N.G.*)

External view of the Paul III Loggia.

Gerolamo Siciolante, *Hadrian Burning the Promissory Notes Signed by the Roman People*, fresco. Paul III Loggia.

Gerolamo Siciolante, *Ideal Reconstruction of Hadrian's Mausoleum*, fresco. Paul III Loggia.

the mausoleum itself, seen beyond a military figure who has his back to us (perhaps the emperor himself). On the barrel vault one can see traces of the crest of Paul III. Continuing anti-clockwise beyond the loggia, one now passes along the **Uncovered Walkway**, bound by the external walls built in 1657 for the Chigi pope Alexander VII to close off the western side of the Castle. This walkway passes by four rooms now used for catering facilities and to house the museum's collection of weapons.

The Castle Armoury
This small collection of antique weapons aims to illustrate the sort of arms used in the battles which involved Castel Sant'Angelo; the focus is more on the historical and documentary value of the pieces rather than their individual aesthetic qualities or their specific associations. When the Castel Sant'Angelo Museum was first set up, it was intended the place

should house a large collection of such weaponry; after all, this was the period immediately after Rome's annexation by the Kingdom of Italy, and in such a fervently patriotic climate there was a clear desire to celebrate the military events that had made the city once more the capital of a nation. Nor should it should not be forgotten that at the time Castel Sant'Angelo was still a fortress, and the first museum to be housed here was that of the Military Engineering Corps (the first Curator, Borgatti— whose taste for "atmospheric" museum design has been amply discussed in this guide—was also a general of that Corps). All of these factors led to numerous rooms of the Castle being filled with arms and weaponry, forming an often "heterogeneous" collection that was intended to conjure up an idea (Borgatti's idea) of what the Castle must have been like in its days of greatest splendour.

Pieces were brought here from some of the most important collections in Italy—for example, the Castello di Gradara collection, or that which had been housed in the former Museo Artistico Industriale [Museum of Industrial Crafts]. Exhibited alongside the various artefacts discovered during excavation and restoration work on the Castle itself, these pieces were intended to chart the development of weaponry from the dawn of history up to the contemporary age.

In recent years, the more historically exact criteria now favoured in such reconstructions have led the curators to review the layout of the collection. This review started with a full study of individual pieces and the drawing-up of a detailed catalogue. Thereafter, it was decided that the displays within Castel Sant'Angelo should focus on the pieces found

n or near the Castle itself, given
that these made a fundamental
contribution to understanding
not only the great historical events
in which the fortress had played
a role but also the details of daily
life within the garrison.
The present-day exhibition
occupies four rooms. The first
contains weapons dating from
the nineteenth and the first
decades of the twentieth century
and used either by the army
of the Papal States (which held
Castel Sant'Angelo until 1870)
or the Army of the newly-unified
Italy. The more significant pieces
include the classical-style helmets
and the uniforms of the Guardia
Civica set up by Pius IX in 1848;
there is also the uniform of
Herman Kanzler, who was general
of the papal forces when Rome
fell to the Italian troops of general
Raffaele Cadorna. The weapons
of the Italian army illustrate the
various changes that organisation
went through in the period
1870–1900, as the various pre-
Unification and Garibaldi units
were absorbed by the army of the
Kingdom of Piedmont. Though
the exhibition focuses on the
Corazzieri [Cuirassiers] and *Granatieri*
[Grenadiers]—the regiments most
actively involved in the fighting
around Rome—one very rare piece
here is the uniform of the Piacenza
Hussars; a pre-Unification cavalry
unit formed mainly by Hungarian
exiles, this maintained its Austro-
Hungarian uniforms and structure
even after being absorbed
by the army of a United Italy.
In the second room is a
sixteenth-century wheel-lock
arquebus made for the Farnese
family; note the fine engraving
on the barrel and the decoration
of the case. There are also two
splendid pistols with inlays:
the first, dating from the late
sixteenth century, comes from
the Castle of Gradara, whilst
the second was made by a Saxon

gunsmith of the seventeenth
century. The third room has
various firearms and pieces that
reflect the growing importance
of gunpowder, which was first
introduced on a wide scale
in the sixteenth century and
totally changed offensive and
defensive strategies and tactics
during the course of the
seventeenth (see, for example, the
alterations in the fortifications
of Castel Sant'Angelo itself which
have already been described).

Buckler in boiled hide and wood, late sixteenth century. From the Castello di Gradara Collection, Museo Nazionale di Castel Sant'Angelo.

Italian-made buckler, decorated with trophies and figures around the central stud, second half of the sixteenth century. Museo Nazionale di Castel Sant'Angelo.

German-made cylindrical helmet dating from the beginning of the fourteenth century. Generally known as the "Bolzano Helmet," after the area of production, this one of the most interesting pieces in the collection. Museo Nazionale di Castel Sant'Angelo.

Standard of the Bombardiers of Castel Sant'Angelo. Museo Nazionale di Castel Sant'Angelo.

The exhibits include the accessories used in loading firearms and cannon, swords which have been modified to include firearms, numerous pistols, and a splendid *buttafuoco* [bombard cannon] dating from the fifteenth century. There is also the standard of the Confraternità dei Bombardieri di Castel Sant'Angelo, probably made around the middle of the eighteenth century for the Chapel of Santa Barbara in the church of Santa Maria Traspontina. The last room is dedicated to the history of the Castle, with shields, helmets and swords used by the soldiers who defended the fortress in the fifteenth-to-eighteenth centuries; there are also some of the weapons of the lansquenets who took part in the Sack of Rome in 1527. Note a helmet adorned with the Barberini coat-of-arms; a half suit of armour dating from the seventeenth century; a shield decorated with a depiction of Constantine at the Battle of Milvian Bridge; and a buckler with etched decoration dating from the second half of the sixteenth century.

Moving back across the diametrical ramp built for Alexander VI, one passes over the drawbridge and under the archway into the entrance. To the right is a room now closed off with an iron grating; inside one can see Mariano Borgatti's "re-creation" of a sixteenth-century guardhouse, complete with antique helmets and weapons. Once outside, a few steps bring one to the so called **"marcia ronda"** [patrol path] that leads up to the top of the outer walls. Passing along these battlements, where the sentries were protected by tall merlons, one can visit the four polygonal bastions, which were extensively studied (but also extensively "restored") at the beginning of the twentieth century. Once on the battlements, one moves to the right towards the **San Matteo Bastion**, one of those three (the others being the San Luca and the San Marco Bastions) whose present state is the result of centuries of accumulations and alterations. All three of these appear rather similar, even if the size of the polygonal walls

and the structure and height of the crowning battlements vary. None of them, however, still has that small central tower raised in each bastion by Nicolas V in the period 1447–55: in fact, the San Matteo Bastion never had one at all, and the towers on the sites of the other bastions were demolished in the seventeenth century (that which one can see in the San Giovanni Bastion is, as we shall see, the result of the reconstruction carried out by Borgatti at the beginning of the twentieth century). Documentary records, excavations and the evidence brought to light by recent restoration work have enabled scholars to trace the history of the building and adaptation of these bastions. The first fortifications were the above-mentioned towers which Nicholas V had built in the period 1447–55 at three of the corners of the basement to the Roman mausoleum in order to strengthen the fortress's defences against the newly-introduced siege cannon (as has been said, the exception was the corner now occupied by the San Matteo Bastion). Then, between 1492 and 1503, the Borgia pope Alexander VI had the polygonal walls built that still form the core of the bastions' structure. The external wall, which stood as high as the Passetto di Borgo, enclosed the Nicholas V towers, forming a defensive structure of two levels, which could house cannon. Later, in 1559–65, Pius IV raised the battlements of the Borgia walls to the height of the "patrol path," and modified the positioning of the cannons; the result of this work was that the Nicolas V towers were now entirely hidden within the polygonal perimeter wall. And finally, Urban VIII filled in the areas created as a result of the work ordered by Pius IV and ordered further modifications that made the bastions even more solid but altered their outward appearance. A further section of the patrol path brings one now to the **San Marco Bastion** which, as has already been said, still shows clear traces of the various changes to its fortifications. On the outside wall one can still see some of the openings of the sixteen radial compartments opened up by Pius IV to house cannon, as well as the papal coat-of-arms raised to mark the conclusion of that work in 1556. The battlements themselves, which jut forward on massive

Reconstruction of a guard house at the entrance to the Alexander VI ramp.

San Marco Bastion, detail of the outer wall. The two large corbels in travertine at the first arch of the Passetto show the height of this and the other bastions at the time of Alexander VI (late fifteenth century). The upper corbels, just under the railing, show the height to which the structure was raised during the papacy of Pius IV.

The facade of the Clement X Armoury, seen from the patrol path between the bastions.

The San Marco Bastion and the Passetto di Borgo. In the walls of the bastion one can see one of the windows that provided light for the rooms Pius IV had built to house the gunners.

corbels of travertine, are also the result of changes made by the Medici pope. It was this bastion which linked up with the protected passageway from the Vatican known as the "Passetto di Borgo." Passing from here on to the **San Luca Bastion**, one can see on one's right the Courtyard of the Condemned and the facade of the building known as the Clement X Armoury. This square-plan structure stands three storeys

above ground level, two of the floors being linked by internal staircases to the old Nicholas V tower which is no longer visible because entirely enveloped by the bastion. Facing westwards, towards St. Peter's, the curved facade of the armoury bears four coats-of-arms and a plaque which tells us that for the Jubilee of 1675 Clement X had this building renovated to serve as a new armoury and prison. The side onto the courtyard was once porticoed, but then bricked in to create the Chapel of the Condemned (which, as we have already seen, is now the Museum bookshop).

The tour of the battlements now brings one to the **San Giovanni Bastion**, alongside which stands a small building in which Borgatti set up a "sixteenth-century armsmith's shop." A first glance reveals the features that distinguish this from the other bastions—the very pronounced battlements and the central tower—which are all the result of restoration work carried out in the first decades of the twentieth century. When, towards the end of the nineteenth century, proposals were put forward for the construction of a riverside drive which would have required extensive demolition of some of the remaining fortifications of Castel Sant'Angelo, the various ministries responsible for the structure—the Ministry of War, the Ministry of Education, etc.—were galvanised into commissioning serious study of the bulwarks; and while perhaps not meeting current standards of scholarly rigour, it was this work that would underline the historical value of the building, thus avoiding any risk of its destruction. Carried out under the direction of Mariano Borgatti, the excavations unearthed traces of the Nicholas V tower, the Borgia foundations for the polygonal walls and the reinforcements of the fortifications that had been added during the sixteenth and seventeenth century. Shortly afterwards, Borgatti embarked on the restoration that would transform Castel Sant'Angelo into a National Museum of the Military Engineering Corps, throwing himself into the task of reviving the former splendour of the building. For him that splendour was at its greatest during the sixteenth century, before the work carried out by Pius IV and Urban VIII—which, in Borgatti's own words, "strengthened the fabric but undermined the aesthetic qualities" of the Castle.

As has already been mentioned, his ideas as to what Castel Sant'Angelo had actually looked like were strongly opposed by the City Department of Antiquities and Fine Arts, which denounced his work on the Castle as arbitrary. Yet though he was forced to cut back the scale of his initial projects, Borgatti did manage to intervene substantially in the structure of the San Giovanni Bastion, which was almost entirely demolished and "rebuilt" as Borgatti assumed it to have been in the days of Alexander VI, with the Nicholas V tower and battlements resting on massive (newly built) corbels. (*L.B.*)

Having completed one's tour, one now continues to the exit along the Paul III ramp that leads into the Saviour Courtyard. In niches alongside there are two noteworthy marble busts: the expressionistic (perhaps posthumous) *Bust of Hadrian*, which reflects a type of official portrait that dates from the very beginning of his reign, and the more interesting *Bust of a Male Figure in Toga*, in whose damaged features one can still recognise a portrait of Julius Caesar. It has been argued this latter is one of those portrait busts commissioned in Rome and other Italian cities by the

Bust of Hadrian in a niche on the Paul III ramp.

The San Giovanni Bastion.

prosperous middle classes during the Late Republican period (works which took their inspiration from the portraits of Caesar); however, it is now generally accepted that the bust dates from the middle of the second century AD and was inspired by the same political/ideological purpose as those reproduction busts of Caesar that appeared in the cycles of imperial portraits in the Trajan Forum. (*N.G.*)

The structure commonly referred to as the Passetto di Borgo was a covered walk-way built to guarantee the pope's safety as he moved from the Vatican to Castel Sant'Angelo; hence, its creation is closely linked with the transformation of Hadrian's Mausoleum into a papal fortress. Thanks to the restoration work carried out for the 2000 Jubilee, one can now walk along some of the passageway, entering at the San Marco Bastion through a doorway surmounted by a cupola. From the walls of the bastion one can easily understand the layout of the Passetto, which runs along a fortified wall for around eight hundred metres to the papal palaces of the Vatican. This observation point also gives an extraordinary view of the district around St. Peter's, a place radically transformed by the City Planning Scheme of 1931 and yet still bearing traces of centuries of growth and development. In effect, one cannot fully understand the creation and function of the Passetto itself unless one looks briefly at the history of the district that lies to the west of the Castle, for only then can one appreciate the strategic importance of the defensive structures across which the covered passageway was built.

Hadrian built his mausoleum in a scarcely-populated area known as the *Ager Vaticanus*, a wide flat zone stretching from the right bank of the Tiber to the hills of the Vatican. The link with the city proper was guaranteed by the *Pons Neronis* (which stood at the site of the present-day Ponte Vittorio Emanuele); and the internal

Robert Eaton, *The Basilica of St. Peter's and the Passetto di Borgo*, c. 1855. City Photographic Archives, Rome.

The different phases in the construction of the Passetto di Borgo: the blocks of tufa date from the sixth century (Totila) and the brick wall was built from the ninth century onwards (starting with Leo IV).

oad system of the area hinged around the *Via Triumphalis*, which ran north-south cross the *Pons Neronis* to modern-day Monte Mario, and the *Via Cornelia*, which ran ast-west towards the site of St. Peter's (the last part of this porticoed road coin-ided roughly with the lay-out of the present-day Via della Conciliazione). The ntire zone contained various imperial gardens and numerous burial areas, as ell as such large public buildings as the Circus of Nero and Caligula (probably he site of St. Peter's martyrdom). The area around the site of the Castle itself was •ccupied by the so-called *Prata Neronis* (Garden of Nero), where a number of those ho fled here from the terrible fire of 64 AD chose to make their homes rather han return to the other side of the river.

he entire area lay outside the city walls built by emperor Aurelian in 271 AD, nd the sole defences of the zone were the river itself and the massive structure of Iadrian's Mausoleum.

he prestige of the *Prata* area increased when the emperor Constanine decided to aise a basilica on the site of St. Peter's martyrdom, within the necropolis that •acked onto the Circus of Nero. That church was consecrated in 326 AD and thus he area was soon attracting pilgrims from all over Europe. Over the years, a •umber of structures were built around St. Peter's by various foreign communi-ies anxious to provide services and assistance to their fellow-countrymen who •ad made the long trip to Rome; including at least one church, an inn and very •ften a hospital, such structures became known as *scholae*.

he first fortification of the area came in the sixth century and was built by the)strogoth king Totila, who had settled his troops in the *Prata Neronis* and raised a •efensive wall here against the troops of the Emperor of the East, Justinian. The Ierman name for this fortified area was *Burg*, which is traditionally given as the •rigin of the present name for district, Borgo.

\ short distance away, near St. Peter's, the first episcopal residences had mean-/hile been built; however, these were mainly service structures for the faithful,

Mario Cartaro, *Plan of Rome*, 1576, engraving. Drawn shortly after the construction of the Pius IV walls, this plan of the city shows the Passetto di Borgo running from the fortress (upper right) to the Vatican, passing alongside the *Platea Sancti Petri* (St. Peter's Square), where Bernini's colonnade is yet to be built. To the left one can see the new defensive walls to the north of the city. The *Civitas Pia* would occupy the area between those new walls and the Passetto.

given that the popes and bishops continued to live in the Lateran area.

In 800 Charlemagne was crowned Holy Roman Emperor in the Basilica of St. Peter's, and fully understanding the symbolic importance of these buildings within the very heart of Christian Rome, chose to make this area his headquarters for the time he stayed in the city. In order to guarantee his safety here, however, he strengthened the fortifications that had been raised by Totila.

But in spite of this work, the Saracens were able to sack the outer city in 846, sweeping through the Borgo area and all the other districts that lay outside the walls built for Aurelian. As a result, Pope Leo IV undertook the full reconstruction of the district and an extension of its defences.

With the assistance of the Holy Roman Emperor, Lothair, the pontiff transformed the Borgo into what became known as the "Leonine Citadel," dominated by the Castle and enclosed by new walls which, incorporating part of the old Totila walls, ran from the mausoleum to the basilica and then towards the Tiber. These new walls were some five metres high and topped by battlements; the first stretch, of around 800 metres in length, ran from the Castle to St. Peter's and it was on this that the Passetto would be created. Those who wish to follow that covered pathway, as far as the remains of Porta Castello, can still see the tufa blocks that were used in the Totila walls (above which were raised the sections built in the Middle Ages).

Within this defensive barrier, the district continued to develop and grow in population, with the main activities here still being linked to assistance for the faithful. One of the main spurs to growth was the hospital of Santo Spirito in Sassia, built at the behest of Innocence III at the end of the thirteenth century on the ruins of the old *Schola Saxonum* (and repeatedly altered over the centuries to come). The long block of the hospital, surmounted by an octagonal lantern, can be seen when one looks towards the bend in the Tiber from the parapets of the San Marco Bastion.

The defensive nature of the Passetto wall was further confirmed at the end of the thirteenth century by Nicholas III, who aimed to make the area secure as the permanent home of the papacy, by now firmly established in the Vatican: the Leo IV walls were consolidated and, in a stroke of genius, the pope had a covered walkway built along those walls from the Vatican to the Castel Sant'Angelo, so that the pope could find safe refuge there in situations of danger. Hence, once the papacy moved to the Vatican, the Passetto became an integral part of the defence system that guaranteed the safety of the bishops of Rome.

With the spread of the new Renaissance theories regarding urban development, the popes of the fifteenth century put great effort into adapting the layout of the

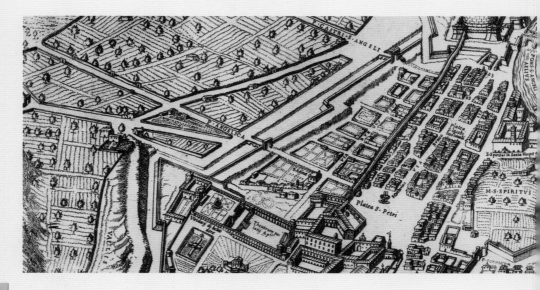

Borgo area; just as the determination to make Castel Sant'Angelo a fittingly princely residence for the pontiff led to the creation of papal apartments, it also resulted in the modernisation of the district gathered around the walls of the fortress. Nicholas V's plans for the area envisaged three main arterial roads running from the Castle to the Vatican: Borgo Santo Spirito, nearest the river and alongside the hospital of the same name; Porticus Maior, subsequently known as Borgo Vecchio, running along the route of the ancient Via Cornelia towards the central portal of the basilica; and Via Sancta, later known as Borgo Nuovo, leading to the palaces of the Vatican. Between 1471 and 1484 Sixtus IV would then promote the construction of magnificent residences to replace the crumbling medieval structures, a process of refurbishment that was further consolidated when work began on the new basilica of St. Peter's in 1506.

Throughout this period, the work on the defences in this area of the city focused mainly on strengthening those already existing around the Leonine Citadel. Boniface IX had commissioned reconstruction work at the end of the fourteenth/beginning of the fifteenth century, but it was in the second half of the fifteenth century that Nicholas V and Alexander VI would undertake extensive consolidation work: the Borgia pope was responsible for the new walkway with merlons above the covered fourteenth-century Passetto, to which was now added two square towers (one still extant) to defend the ancient Porta Viridaria (now Porta Castello). This new structure of the Passetto would later save the life of Clement VII, who managed to escape to Castel Sant'Angelo during the terrible Sack of Rome in 1527 by German lansquenets.

The defensive importance of the Passetto, however, declined at the end of the sixteenth century, when Pius IV commissioned the building of a wall running to the Prata Neronis area; linking up with the pentagonal fortifications the same pope had had added to Castel Sant'Angelo, this new wall extended further northward than the Leo IV city walls and thus became the outer fortifications on that side of the city. Now, therefore, the Passetto became the southern boundary of an area whose development was promoted by Pius IV, hence its name of Civitas Pia. This new district arose from 1565 onwards, bound to the north by the modern ramparts, to the south by the Passetto, to the east by the polygonal walls of Castel Sant'Angelo and to the west by the buildings of the Vatican. At this point, therefore, the wall along which the Passetto ran had become an obstacle to traffic between the Civitas and the Borgo, and seven openings where cut through it, which are now occupied by modern roads (in the keystones to the arches over these openings one can see the crest of the Medici pope).

Work on the area would continue in the seventeenth century, when in the period 1656–67 Bernini worked on the creation of the monumental square in front of the basilica: the work on the colonnades required the demolition of numerous buildings that over the centuries had grown up around St. Peter's

But the most flagrant work in this area was that which resulted from the 1931 Urban Development Plan, which completely destroyed the old urban fabric of the Borgo: the would-be monumental scenography of the Via della Conciliazione— so in keeping with the tastes of the day—cut right through the tightly-knit weave of the medieval district and its irregular pattern of streets.

Visitors to the Passetto can now gain access to the covered walkway and walk along the upper ramparts, from which one can appreciate the entire layout of the Vatican area.

At the beginning, the route runs above the gardens of the Parco Adrianeo, laid out around the sixteenth-century pentagonal perimeter walls of Castel Sant'Angelo. Looking towards the river, one can see Piazza Pia and the monumental approach to Via della Conciliazione, which stand upon the area that up until 1860 was occupied by part of the defences of the Borgo district.

Continuing along the wall, one passes over the various gateways opened up during the course of the centuries: Porta Castello, Porta d'Orfeo, Porta Palline and, near the Vatican, Porta del Mascarino. From here one has a panoramic view of the entire district of St. Peter's, with the basilica to one's left and the modern-day Prati district—on the site of the old Civitas Pia—to one's right. (L.B.)

The Popes
of Castel Sant'Angelo

Gregory I (St. Gregory the Great) 590–604

Born into an aristocratic Roman family, he was appointed Prefect of that city at an early age. He later took religious orders, continuing his diplomatic career at the Court of Constantinople. Once elected pope, his skill as a mediator enabled him to maintain good relations with Byzantium, the Franks and the Visigoths, and to promote the conversion of the Brittany area to Christianity. He reformed the Roman liturgy and supported the nascent monastic movement of St. Benedict.

Boethius, *Pope Gregory I between the Fathers of the Church Jerome and Augustine*, diptych. Musei Civici, Brescia.

Leo IV, 847–855

Famous for his rectitude and asceticism, he was elected pope the very day that his predecessor died. He immediately set about trying to repair the damage in Rome caused by the Saracen raids of 846, as well as setting up fortresses along the Tyrrhenian coast. In Rome itself, he drew on the assistance of the emperor Lothair to fortify the area around Castel Sant'Angelo, creating the

Pope Leo IV (?) in a fresco from the lower basilica of San Clemente in Rome.

so-called "Leonine Citadel." The labour force for this project included the Saracens who had been captured at the naval battle of Ostia in 849, when a League formed by the pontiff himself had defeated the raiders' ships.

Nicholas III (Giovanni Gaetano Orsini), 1277–1280

One of the few popes who was able to resist political interference by the French king Charles I Anjou. His family were the actual owners of Castel Sant'Angelo, and thus the Castle returned into papal hands after centuries of feudal anarchy. He commissioned the Passetto di Borgo to guarantee his safety.

Nicholas III Holding a Model of the Sancta Santorum, thirteenth century, fresco (detail). Holy Staircase, Chapel of the Sancta Santorum, Rome.

Boniface IX (Pietro Tomacelli), 1389–1404

Elected pope in one of the most troubled periods in the Church's history, when Gregory XI's decision to transfer the papal court to Avignon had given rise to the Great Schism. Like his predecessor, Urban VI, he insisted upon the need for the pope to be resident in Rome, but he did not manage to resolve the deep split between the two factions.

Nicholas V (Tommaso Parentucelli), 1447–1455

This skilled diplomat reached an agreement

with the emperor Frederick III, whom he crowned in Rome in 1452. He also promoted the re-organisation of the Papal States and subjugated Bologna. Surrounded by a court of erudite scholars and humanists, it was he who took the decision to demolish the old basilica of St. Peter's to build a new one. A passionate bibliophile, he founded the Vatican Library and commissioned work from such artists as Benozzo Gozzoli, Fra Angelico, Piero della Francesca and Andrea del Castagno.

Alexander VI (Rodrigo Borgia), 1492–1503

The image passed down by history is of a corrupt man who was a slave to his passions and dedicated to his two children, Cesare and Lucrezia. However, whilst looking after his own interests, he also followed a multifaceted policy as Head of the Church, aiming to protect Italy from the expansionism of the foreign States which hoped to take advantage of the instability that had resulted from the death of Lorenzo de Medici. He promoted the union of Christian rulers against the Turks and called a consistory to undertake reform of the Church.

Circle of Melozzo da Forlì, *Portrait of Alexander VI*, oil on panel. Vatican Museum, Vatican City.

Julius II (Giuliano della Rovere), 1503–1513

Of humble origins, he became a monk in the Franciscan Order, whose Father General was his uncle (the future Sixtus IV). Appointed cardinal for his military rather than religious virtues he confirmed these gifts when in 1486 he led an army that drove back the Aragonian forces from the gates of Rome. During the papacy of Alexander VI he had to go into exile, and when pope himself issued a bull against simony; but his sale of indulgences to pay for the work on St. Peter's (he had laid the foundation stone himself) would arouse the first protests of Martin Luther. A true Renaissance prince, he was a great patron of the arts, calling to Rome such artists as Bramante and Michelangelo (from whom he commissioned the work in the Sistine Chapel and on his own monumental tomb), as well as Raphael, commissioned to decorate the famous Stanze in the Vatican.

Raphael, *Portrait of Julius II*, 1511–12, oil on panel. Uffizi Gallery, Florence.

Leo X (Giovanni de' Medici), 1513–1521

Second son of Lorenzo the Magnificent, he was educated by the great humanists of the Medici court. Despite his balanced policy in handling the foreign powers, he could not prevent Italy being divided up. Little interested in spiritual matters, he found himself having to deal with the earthquake caused by Martin Luther's Reformation.

understanding neither its importance nor deep moral motivations. He was a patron of such writers and artists as Bonifacio Bembo, Francesco Guicciardini, Michelangelo and Raphael (whose commission to work on the Stanze he re-confirmed). His papacy coincides with the most glorious period of the Renaissance, which would end so dramatically with the Sack of Rome.

Raphael, *Portrait of Leo X and Two Cardinals*, 1518–19, oil on panel. Uffizi Gallery, Florence.

Clement VII (Giulio de' Medici), 1523–1534

His papacy would see one of the most terrible events in the history of Rome, the sack of the city by the lansquenets of the Hapsburg emperor Charles V in 1527, during which around ten thousand people were killed and even the papal tombs were ripped open in the search for treasure; the pope himself escaped by passing along the Passetto di Borgo to take refuge in Castel

Sebastiano del Piombo, *Portrait of Clement VII*, c. 1526, oil on canvas. Capodimonte Museum, Naples.

Sant'Angelo. The imperial troops were finally withdrawn after the papacy agreed to swingeing terms: the surrender of the fortresses of Ostia, Civitavecchia and Civita Castellana, the ceding of Modena, Parma and Piacenza, and the payment of 400,000 ducats.

Paul III (Alexander Farnese), 1534–1549

Following a policy of shameless nepotism, he placed members of his family in numerous key positions, even giving them control of a "state" formed of the territories of Parma and Piacenza. He was, however, also the pope who promoted the Council of Trent, the Church's response to the spread of Protestantism. In order to restore the fortunes of Catholicism, he also supported the foundation of the Order of the Jesuits and of the Roman Inquisition. Imbued with humanist culture, he undertook a magnificent re-building of Rome, well aware of the propaganda benefits of investment in art.

Titian, *Portrait of Paul III with his Nephews Alessandro and Ottavio Farnese*, 1543, oil on canvas. Capodimonte Museum, Naples.

Pius IV (Giovanni Angelo Medici) 1560–1565

Assisted by his nephew—the cardinal Federico Borromeo—he brought the Council of Trent to its conclusion, thus providing the momentum for the Catholic Counter-Reformation. In a return to austerity, the Church

undertook a new campaign of spiritual and moral values, intending to re-conquer the minds of the faithful and spread Catholicism through the new lands of the colonies.

Clement VIII (Ippolito Aldobrandini), 1592–1605

A rigid authoritarian, he fought a relentless campaign against brigandage in the area around Rome. He condemned to death the parricide Beatrice Cenci, in spite of her young age and the many attenuating circumstances to her crime; he also ordered that Giordano Bruno be burnt at the stake. His Counter-Reformation moralism made him favour writers who stood as propagandists for the Church: for example, he had Torquato Tasso crowned with laurel in a ceremony on the Campidoglio.

Urban VIII (Maffeo Barberini), 1623–1644

From an aristocratic Florentine family, he began his ecclesiastical career after studying Law. He was closely linked with the Accademia dei Lincei and shared its members' passionate interest in the discoveries being made by Galileo, who would dedicate his *Saggiatore* to this pope. However, the precepts of the Council of Trent, and anxiety over the spread of heresy, ultimately led him to con-

Pietro da Cortona, *Portrait of Urban VIII*, 1626–27, oil on canvas. Capitoline Picture Gallery, Rome.

demn the scientist and also take measures against the philosopher Tommaso Campanella. An enthusiastic lover of the arts, he was patron to Bernini and the many other artists who would adorn Rome with fountains, palaces and new city squares.

Pius VI (Giovanni Angelo Braschi), 1775–1799

Elected pope with the support of France, he broke with that country after the advent of the Revolution in 1789. Before that earthquake, however, he had attempted to introduce cautious financial, legal and judicial reforms into the rather sclerotic Papal States; one famous project was the land-reclamation work in the Agro Romano. A patron of the arts, he further adorned the city and extended the Vatican Museum. In 1796 he was forced to recognise the French Republic, but he was still kept a prisoner and ultimately taken to France (where he died). (*L.B.* and *N.G.*)

Chronology

121–130 AD Work begins on the construction of Hadrian's Mausoleum and the Pons Aelius.

134 The Opening of the Pons Aelius.

138 Hadrian dies at Baia and is buried at Pozzuoli.

139 Hadrian's body is transferred to the mausoleum.

217 Caracalla is the last emperor to be buried in the mausoleum.

271 The emperor Aurelian starts work on the new city walls.

313 The emperor Constantine grants freedom of worship to the Christians.

330 The capital of the empire is transferred from Rome to Byzantium.

410 The Goths of Alaric sack Rome.

476 Odoacer deposes Romulus Augustulus, the last emperor of the West.

493–526 Theodoric, king of the Ostrogoths, is in Rome. His name thence becomes linked to the mausoleum, which documents refer to as *Carcer Theoderici* or *Domus Theoderici*.

535–553 The Graeco-Gothic War, with the Goths of Witgis and Totila fighting the forces of the emperor of the East, Justinian, for control of Italy.

547 In the area around the mausoleum, king Totila establishes his military base, known as *Burg*.

590–604 Papacy of St. Gregory the Great.

608–614 Papacy of Boniface VI.

800 Charlemagne is crowned Holy Roman Emperor in St. Peter's by Pope Leo III.

846 The Saracens sack the basilicas that lie outside the Rome city walls built by Aurelian.

849 Defeat of the Saracens at Ostia.

852 Foundation of the Leonine Citadel.

887 End of the Carolingian empire.

1073–1085 Gregory VII, determined defender of papal autonomy, excommunicates the emperor Henry IV.

1152 Frederic I Barbarossa becomes king of Germany. Pope Adrian IV resists the Rome Commune's assertions of independence and lives besieged within Castel Sant'Angelo.

1176 The Lega Lombarda defeats Barbarossa at Legnano. The pope's temporal power over the Papal States is recognised.

1277–1280 Papacy of Nicholas III. Construction of the Passetto di Borgo.

1311–1376 Pope Clement V moves the papacy to Avignon.

1378 The Great Schism in the Western Church.

1379 The Romans attempt to destroy Castel Sant'Angelo.

1389–1404 Papacy of Boniface IX (Pietro Tomacelli).

1417 The Western Schism comes to an end.

1431–1447 Papacy of Eugenius IV (Gabriele Condulmer).

1447–1455 Papacy of Nicolas V (Tommaso Parentucelli)

1458–1464 Papacy of Pius II (Enea Silvio de Piccolomini)

1471–1484 Papacy of Sixtus IV (Francesco della Rovere)

1492 Christopher Columbus lands in America; Lorenzo the Magnificent dies.

1492–1503 Papacy of Alexander VI (Rodrigo Borgia).

1494 Troops of the French king Charles VIII in Italy; Ludovico il Moro, Lord of Milan, and Piero de Medici, Lord of Florence, are deposed.

1503–1513 Papacy of Julius II (Giuliano della Rovere).

1513–1521 Papacy of Leo X (Giovanni de' Medici).

1520 Martin Luther publicly burns the papal bull of Leo X excommunicating him.

1523–1534 Papacy of Clement VII (Giulio de' Medici)

1527 The army of emperor Charles V sacks Rome. Clement VII takes refuge in Castel Sant'Angelo.

1534–1549 Papacy of Paul III (Alessandro Farnese).

1555–1559 Papacy of Paul IV (Giovanni Pietro Carafa).

1560–1565 Papacy of Pius IV (Giovanni Angelo Medici).

1585–1590 Sixtus renovates Rome and re-organises the Papal States.

1592–1606 Papacy of Clement VIII (Ippolito Aldobrandini).

1623–1644 Papacy of Urban VIII (Maffeo Barberini).

1655–1667 Papacy of Alexander VII (Fabio Chigi).

1798 French troops conquer Rome. Pius VI dies in exile.

20 September 1870 Porta Pia is taken. Rome becomes the capital of Italy.

Bibliography

Letizia Abbondanza,
"Osservazioni su alcuni
rinvenimenti dell'area
di Castel Sant'Angelo,"
in *Adriano e il suo mausoleo*,
exhibition catalogue
(Rome 1998), Milan
1998. pp. 39–49.

*Adriano e il suo mausoleo.
Studi, indagini e interpretazioni*,
European project
"All Roads Lead to
Rome," exhibition
catalogue (Rome 1998),
Milan 1998.

*Gli affreschi di Paolo III
a Castel Sant'Angelo. Progetto
ed esecuzione 1543–1548*,
exhibition catalogue
(Rome 1981–1982),
Rome 1981.

Maria Maddalena
Alessandro,
"Mausoleo di Adriano,"
in *ROMArcheologica*, 7,
2000, pp. 51–59.

Le ali di Dio, edited by
Marco Bussagli, Marco
D'Onofrio, www.enec.it.

Filippa M. Aliberti
Gaudioso, "Un'antologia
del Manierismo romano;
Storia e mito negli
affreschi di Perino;
Dopo Perino, una nuova
arte," in *Roma il Castel
Sant'Angelo*, GrandTour
FMR, limited edition,
Milan 1990, pp. 66–76.

Giulio Carlo Argan,
Bruno Contardi,
Michelangelo architetto, Milan
1990, pp. 64–66.

*L'armeria storica di Castel
Sant'Angelo*, edited by
Glauco Angeletti,
Rome 1991.

*Breve visita al Museo Nazionale
di Castel Sant'Angelo*,
Milan 1998.

Giuliano Briganti,
Gaspar van Wittel, Milan
1996, pp. 178–87.

David Alan Brown,
San Girolamo nella selva,

in *Lorenzo Lotto. Il genio
inquieto del Rinascimento*,
exhibition catalogue
(Bergamo 1998),
edited by David Alan
Brown, Peter Humfrey,
Mauro Lucco, Milan
1998, pp. 94–96, n. 8.

Arnaldo Bruschi,
"L'armonica cittadella
del papa umanista;
Alessandro VI, il
fortificatore; Tra
Bramante e Antonio da
Sangallo; La 'Chamera
del Papa'; Una nuova
cinta contro il turco,"
in *Roma il Castel Sant'Angelo*,
cit., pp. 40–65.

Vannella Carrelli,
Rosaria Punzi,
*I Bambini alla Scoperta
di Roma da Castel Sant'Angelo
a San Pietro*, Rome 1997.

*Castel Sant'Angelo. Immagini-
rilievi*, edited by Cesare
Cundari, Rome 2000.

Benvenuto Cellini,
Vita, edited by Ettore
Camesasca, Milan 1985.

André Chastel,
"Et in Italia ego," in
Roma il Castel Sant'Angelo,
cit., pp. 11–23.

Filippo Coarelli,
Roma, Guide archeologiche
Mondadori, Milan 1994.

Gianluigi Colalucci,
"Relazione del restauro
dell'Arcangelo Michele di
Raffaello da Montelupo,"
in *Studi su Castel Sant'Angelo.
Archivium Arcis 3*, edited
by Liliana Pittarello,
Rome 1991, pp. 172–73.

Maria Letizia Conforto,
"Architetture fantastiche.
Lo spazio invisibile della
città antica: riti, sogni,
funzioni," in *Adriano e il suo
mausoleo*, cit., pp. 93–99.

Bruno Contardi,
"Itinerarium," in *Roma
il Castel Sant'Angelo*, cit.,
pp. 81–91.

Bruno Contardi,
"Il nuovo allestimento

della sezione di sculture
medioevali e moderne,"
in *I grandi progetti di intervento
nel settore dei Beni Culturali*,
Cinisello Balsamo 1990,
pp. 55–61.

Bruno Contardi,
"Raffaello da Montelupo
a Castel Sant'Angelo.
In margine al restauro
dell'Angelo in marmo,"
in *Studi su Castel Sant'Angelo.
Archivium Arcis 3*, cit.,
pp. 167–72.

Maria Grazia D'Amelio,
"Il ponte degli Angeli
a Roma," in *I ponti delle
capitali d'Europa*, edited
by Donatella Calabi,
Claudia Conforti, Milan
2002, pp. 105–17.

Adriana Della Valle,
Daniela Fondi,
Claudio Sterpi,
*Il Passetto e il suo Borgo
nelle immagini del passato
(1875–1939)*, Rome 1997.

C. De Vita,
*Museo Nazionale di Castel
Sant'Angelo. Le Armerie*,
Rome 1979.

Cesare D'Onofrio,
*Gian Lorenzo Bernini
e gli Angeli di Ponte
Sant'Angelo*, Rome 1981.

Cesare D'Onofrio,
*Castel S. Angelo: immagini
e storia*, Rome 1984.

Cesare D'Onofrio,
*Come visitare Castel
Sant'Angelo nella storia
di Roma e del Papato*,
Rome 1988.

Cesare D'Onofrio,
"Il Castel Sant'Angelo;
Adriano, 'Omnium
curiositatum explorator';
Il Castello e l'angelo,"
in *Roma il Castel Sant'Angelo*,
cit., pp. 25–38.

Felipe V. Garín
Llombart, "Alessandro VI
a Roma: cultura
e committenza artistica,"
in *I Borgia*, exhibition
catalogue (Rome
2002–03), Milan 2002,
pp. 119–33.

*Gaspare Vanvitelli e le origini
del vedutismo*, edited by
L. Laureati, L. Trezzani,
exhibition catalogue
(Rome-Venice
2002–03), Rome 2002,
pp. 126–37.

Roberto Gervaso,
*Il Grande Mago. Vita, morte e
miracoli del conte di Cagliostro*,
Milan 2002.

Alessandra Ghidoli Tomei,
*Museo Nazionale di Castel
Sant'Angelo. La quadreria*,
Rome 1979.

Alessandra Ghidoli Tomei,
Marina Mercalli,
*Museo Nazionale di Castel
Sant'Angelo. La Sala Paolina
e la Sala della Biblioteca*,
Rome 1984.

Alessandra Ghidoli
Tomei, "La sala del
Tesoro in Castel
Sant'Angelo: ambiente ed
arredo. Note e riflessioni
in occasione del
restauro," in *Studi su Castel
Sant'Angelo. Archivium Arcis 3*,
cit., pp. 203–19.

Giovanni Ioppolo,
"Ponte Elio. Indagini
e restauri 1994," in *Strade
romane. Ponti e viadotti*,
Rome 1996, pp. 85–102.

Alberto Manodori,
"Memorie sparse del
Mausoleo di Adriano,"
in *Adriano e il suo mausoleo*,
cit., pp. 149–59.

Otto Mazzucato,
*Museo Nazionale di Castel
Sant'Angelo. Le Maioliche*,
Rome 1979.

Otto Mazzucato,
"I pavimenti borgiani,"
in *I Borgia*, cit.,
pp. 168–74

Marina Mercalli,
"Il Mausoleo di Adriano
nelle ricostruzioni
ipotetiche e fantastiche
dal XV al XX secolo,"
in *Adriano e il suo mausoleo*,
cit., pp. 65–92.

Marina Mercalli,
"'Paolo terzo pontefice

nassimo ha trasformato a tomba del Divo Adriano in alta e sacra dimora.' Storia e motivi adrianei negli affreschi dell'Appartamento Farnesiano in Castel Sant'Angelo," in *Adriano e il suo mausoleo*, cit., pp. 255–75.

Emma Nardi, *Castel Sant'Angelo. Struttura e funzioni*, Rome 1992.

Passetto di Borgo. Storia, restauro, progetto, edited by Patrizia Marchetti, Rome 2001.

Anna Maria Pedrocchi, "Dama con liocorno (Giulia Farnese?)," in *I Borgia*, cit., pp. 34–36, n. I.59.

Francesca Petre Antica, "Baccanale," in *I Borgia*, cit., pp. 256–57, n. III.6.

Liliana Pittarello, "Castel Sant'Angelo. Progetti di intervento," in *I grandi progetti di intervento nel settore dei Beni Culturali*, Cinisello Balsamo 1990, pp. 53–55.

Roma il Castel Sant'Angelo, GrandTour FMR, limited edition, Milan 1990.

Il "San Girolamo" di Lorenzo Lotto a Castel Sant'Angelo, edited by Bruno Contardi and Augusto Gentili, exhibition catalogue (Rome 1983), Rome 1983.

Aurora Scotti, "Ponti a confronto: ponte degli Angeli a Roma e ponte Carlo a Praga," in *I ponti delle capitali d'Europa*, cit., pp. 119–29.

Tina Squadrilli, *Castel Sant'Angelo. Una storia lunga diciannove secoli*, Rome 2002.

D.E. Strong, *Late Adrianic Architectural Ornament in Rome*, Paper of the British School at Rome, 21, 1953, pp. 118–51.

Studi su Castel Sant'Angelo. Archivium Arcis 3, edited by Liliana Pittarello, Rome 1991.

Maria Grazia Tolomeo, *Ponte Sant'Angelo*, Rome 1990.

Maria Antonietta Tomei, "La regione Vaticana nell'antichità," in *Adriano e il suo mausoleo*, cit., pp. 23–38.

Maria Antonietta Tomei, "Il Mausoleo di Adriano: la decorazione scultorea," in *Adriano e il suo mausoleo*, cit., pp. 101–14.

La via degli angeli. Il restauro della decorazione scultorea di Ponte Sant'Angelo, edited by Luisa Cardilli Alloisi and Maria Grazia Tolomeo Speranza, Rome 1988.

Marguerite Yourcenar, *Memorie di Adriano seguite dai Taccuini di appunti*, edited by Lidia Storoni Mazzolani, Turin 1988.

Pietro Zampetti, *Lotto*, Bologna 1983, n. 8.

Pietro Zampetti, *Carlo Crivelli*, Florence 1986, pp. 299–301, pls. 106–14.

Pietro Zampetti, Giampiero Donnini, *Gentile e i pittori di Fabriano*, Florence 1992, pp. 221–25.

Federico Zeri, "Cinque schede su Carlo Crivelli," in *Arte Antica e Moderna*, 1961, pp. 17–19.

This volume was printed for Mondadori Electa S.p.A., Milan
by Mondadori Printing S.p.A., Verona in 2008